"Then **Perreault** Said to **Rico...**"

The Best Buffalo Sabres Stories Ever Told

Paul Wieland

TRIUMPH
B O O K S

Library of Congress Cataloging-in-Publication Data

Wieland, Paul, 1938–
"Then Perreault said to Rico..." : the best Buffalo Sabres stories ever told / Paul Wieland.
    p. cm.
  ISBN-13: 978-1-60078-095-0
  ISBN-10: 1-60078-095-4
1. Buffalo Sabres (Hockey team)—History. 2. Hockey teams—United States—New York—History. I. Title.
  GV848.B83W54 2008
  796.962'640974797—dc22

                                    2008034324

This book is available in quantity at special discounts for your group or organization. For further information, contact:

Triumph Books
542 South Dearborn Street
Suite 750
Chicago, Illinois 60605
(312) 939-3330
Fax (312) 663-3557

Printed in U.S.A.
ISBN: 978-1-60078-095-0
Design by Patricia Frey
All photos courtesy of Ron Moscati unless otherwise indicated

Content packaged by Mojo Media, Inc.
Joe Funk: Editor
Jason Hinman: Creative Director

*To Betsy, who has suffered through
every puck along the way.*

table of
contents

foreword

He was there when it happened, so when Paul Wieland goes back to the beginning of the Buffalo Sabres in the National Hockey League, it's part of his personal life story. The following pages describe the meteoric rise of a team that reached the pinnacle for an expansion franchise: appearing in the Stanley Cup Finals after the short span of only five years in the league.

Paul describes in great detail the building of the franchise, including the countless hours invested by people who are no longer with us—Seymour and Norty Knox, Dave Forman, Punch Imlach, Frank Christie, and Ted Darling, to name just a few. These men were the pillars of strength in getting the Buffalo Sabres off the ground and onto the ice.

Paul is able to recount many intimate happenings because of his multifaceted duties with the club in public relations, marketing, and television. His recall of events and friendship with many of the players provides insight to all hockey fans as to how things get done in a professional sports organization. The forming of the French Connection line of Gilbert Perreault, Rick Martin, and Rene Robert is recalled in amazing detail. Other Sabres greats like Jim Schoenfeld, Danny Gare, Mike Foligno, Craig Ramsay, and present Buffalo coach Lindy Ruff are also included in a historic march through time.

I have known Paul Wieland for more than 30 years and I must commend him for his recall of events and attention to detail. In *"Then Perreault Said to Rico..."* Paul takes the reader through the formation of the Sabres. Because he also has been a writer and television producer he has been able to keep his finger on the pulse in producing this book.

—Scotty Bowman

acknowledgments

To the men and women who made the Sabres tick, on and off the ice.

To the players who shared their memories with me.

To John Boutet, who spurred me on.

To Pat Vecchio, who made sense of my words.

To Joel Darling, for his perspective.

To those who have left us, especially Ted Darling, Seymour and Norty Knox, Punch Imlach, and Dave Forman, who all were able to pound some sense into me.

introduction

When I first heard in 1970 that the National Hockey League had awarded an expansion franchise to Buffalo, I was working in New York City in corporate public relations. My family had just moved to a new home in a wooded New Jersey suburban town nearly a two-hour commute from my job in midtown Manhattan. It was our second move in 16 months. The first was from Buffalo to Detroit for a job with an automaker, then a promotion to New York to another division of the company.

My phone rang just one day after Buffalo was informed it was in the NHL. The call came from a newspaper friend of mine from my days as a reporter. He was scouting informally for the new franchise that would have to find a PR person. "Are you interested?" asked my friend, who knew of my passion for the sport both as a player and as a fan.

"I am afraid not," I replied. "My wife would kill me if I came home and suggested we move for the third time in less than 18 months."

On top of that, I wasn't too sure that NHL hockey would work in Buffalo. The city had an old and small arena, Memorial Auditorium. It had been successful in the minor American Hockey League, but only sold out those games in playoff situations. The media in Canada were convinced that Buffalo's chance for success in the NHL hinged on its border location, meaning the team would be supported by Canadian fans from the region now called the Golden Horseshoe (Toronto south and west through Hamilton and Niagara Falls).

Ironically, in my eventual 25 years with the Sabres, our season-ticket base never topped more than 13 percent Canadian.

Buffalo is a Rust Belt city, with a steadily declining population and economic base. But it loves its sports teams, and none more than the Sabres, who on New Year's Day in 2008 drew 71,000 fans for an outdoor game against the Pittsburgh Penguins, and another 11,000 watching the Ice Bowl in their home arena. In the summer of 1970, however, I wasn't the only one who wondered if an NHL team could succeed in my hometown. Boy, was I wrong, and I gladly admit it.

In the midst of a steamy New York summer, I had put the whole matter out of my mind, barely noticing when the team was named the Sabres and when Punch Imlach was hired as the first GM and coach.

I didn't know then that I was fated to move for a third time in less than two years. My executive position in public relations with a major auto company was a job that left me cold except for the money. However, the company had just promoted me to New York City, after only a year in Detroit, so the thought of taking a job with a hockey startup and moving was not a pleasant one for my family.

But my office phone rang again in early August with a call from Buffalo. My newspaper friend, Dick Johnston, told me that the Sabres were begging for the right guy, and in his opinion, I was the right guy. It seems the team had hired someone who Punch found incompatible.

Within three weeks I had convinced my wife it would be nice to return to Buffalo, irritated the hell out of my employer by quitting with a week's notice, and met with the team owners, the Knox brothers. I bought a house over the phone (it was owned by my brother-in-law who needed more space) and figured out what to take to Buffalo's first training camp.

From those first days, with the arrival of Gilbert Perreault until his retirement 17 years later, Perreault was indeed the franchise player, with a career record of 512 goals, 814 assists, and a place in the Hockey Hall of Fame. But he was by no means the only reason the Sabres became a success on and off the ice.

This book is about memories from the men who played, as well as from some of us who watched. Looking back on a franchise that was granted under unusual circumstances (its owners—the Knox brothers—had bailed out the sinking ship in Oakland for a year) I found that every player I spoke with treasured his time in Buffalo because of team camaraderie, the owners, and most of all, the city and its fans.

The Sabres didn't win a Stanley Cup during the career of Gilbert Perreault, but he and his teammates turned Buffalo into one of the best hockey towns in North America.

Chapter 1
The Beginning

"My first goal…everyone remembers their first goal. I can't remember the play, but I remember that it was the game winner."

−Gilbert Perreault

A collage of vintage Sabres memorabilia, including media guides, an early book, a commemorative saber, a Roger Crozier goalie mask, and a team jersey.

The First Training Camp

In 1970, Peterborough, Ontario, Canada, hadn't yet caught the first population wave that has changed the southern edge of the province. Peterborough was a sleepy city of 35,000 in an enclave of lakes and woods. Today it's an exurbia to the 4.5 million living in metropolitan Toronto just 83 miles to the west. The 1970 model Peterborough was a world away from having a big-city feel. It was tidy, almost quaint, and decidedly Anglo-Canadian, except for a Chinese restaurant or two.

The Empress Hotel was the place to stay, the best place to eat. The hotel personality? Upper Canada doughty, stiff-upper-lip rectitude, except when the Toronto Maple Leafs came to stay in early September. Then the Empress was the center of the universe for most young men and boys in town, a place where there was a chance to see and hear Teeder Kennedy, or Eddie Shack, or even Johnny Bower for two weeks or so—get an autograph at the hotel and maybe even as the Leafs left the ice at the Memorial Centre a few blocks away.

But the late summer heat in 1970 was as unusual as the team skating two-a-days in the arena, a team wearing red, white, and blue with an emblem like a Pepsi cap instead of the Leafs' blue and white. Buffalo's NHL sweater emblem was blue, gold, white, and a touch of red, but that first training camp saw the players practice in the uniforms of the Buffalo Bisons, their predecessor in the American Hockey League.

The Leafs were gone, and instead their Stanley Cup–winning coach of just three years before was blowing his whistle at another bunch of players, the spanking-new Buffalo Sabres, who'd joined as the NHL's 13th team coincidentally with the 14th, the Vancouver Canucks.

The Sabres were like expansion teams in pro sports before and since, a roster full of culls, castoffs, close to has-beens, and closer to never-weres, plus a bunch of kids locked onto a big-league dream.

Those first days in the Peterborough arena were hell for

some. Elmer "Moose" Vasko, who'd been a regular on the good Chicago teams of the early 1960s, was 30 pounds overweight and trying for a comeback. To say that Moose labored in the skating drills would be kind. And he knew it within a week, quietly packing up and heading home one warm evening.

Those who remained included a shy French-Canadian with the hint of a cowlick and as deft a pair of hands as any young player available in the world that summer. Gilbert Perreault had been the first overall draft choice by the Sabres that June in Montreal's Queen Elizabeth Hotel, and now he was in the Empress in Peterborough, 250 miles west, a language away from home. "I could understand English, but couldn't speak it very well," said Perreault from his home in his native Victoriaville, Quebec. "But I had a lot of help from my teammates at that first training camp. Especially Gerry Meehan, and Jean Guy Talbot. They took good care of me." That included explaining breakfast menus in the Empress coffee shop to Bert, who at first would just order the "same thing" as the guy sitting next to him, rather than struggle with the language.

"That's true," he said, "but the Junior Canadiens were in the OHL [Ontario Hockey League], so I was around English all the time, and I could get by." Perreault got by, but he was known in his career for some of the most pithy dressing-room quotes in history. Once, after an end-to-end highlight film rush for a goal in Buffalo, a reporter asked Bert to describe his play. His reply: "Puck on stick...I shoot."

Lucky Number 11

George "Punch" Imlach always said he would "rather be lucky than good." He was both in the summer of 1970, a few months after he was hired as general manager and coach of the new Buffalo Sabres. His last success had been winning a Stanley Cup in Toronto in the spring of 1967, a feat not matched by the vaunted and haunted Maple Leafs to this day. Punch's abrasive ways had crossed the Leafs' owners, Stafford Smythe and Harold

George "Punch" Imlach was hired as the first general manager and coach of the Sabres.

Ballard, once too often, and he was out the door after a bad follow-up season to the magic Cup run. The Sabres' young owners, Seymour and Northrup Knox, sons of a scion in New York state's art community and an old-school millionaire, had formed an investors group two years before in an attempt to bring the NHL to Buffalo.

They and several of their richest friends put up the bucks the NHL required, but it was another bundle of cash that got the Knoxes the franchise.

The year before, the Oakland Seals were in desperate financial shape and would fold unless someone bailed the franchise out. That someone was a plural; the brothers Knox provided the cash. The tightly knit Brahmins of the NHL came up with a quid pro quo: allowing Buffalo in the league. Canada's politicians had been clamoring for a Vancouver franchise after the first NHL expansion of six teams took in only American cities. Put Vancouver in with Buffalo and get one and a half Canadian teams. It was a given that Buffalo would serve Canadian fans with its border location. That's the only way Buffalo could survive; so went the common thread in Canada's newspapers.

The Sabres were born, with the team's nickname coming from a contest, ironically won by Toronto documentary film maker Harry Cole. His suggestion was chosen by the Knoxes, and the Wilkinson Sword people rushed to make commemorative sabers with Imlach's signature on the blade. Imlach thus was cast in steel (actually sterling silver) before he even had a Buffalo hockey team to coach.

The Wheel Spins

Imlach's lack of a team to coach was resolved over two days in a flocked wallpaper ballroom of the Queen Elizabeth, converted to hold the NHL's 14 team tables and a curious media contingent.

The first pick in the amateur draft would go to either Buffalo or Vancouver. That first pick would be a consensus one: Gilbert Perreault of the Montreal Junior Canadiens. Perreault was a smooth, strong, and deft center who was head and shoulders above the rest of those draft eligible. He was a "franchise player." The league's scouts were nearly unanimous.

The NHL's president at the time, and for what seemed to his critics like an eternity, was Clarence Campbell, a dour stiff-necked lawyer who had been on the prosecution team at the Nuremburg trials after World War II. Campbell's pursed-lip speaking style and his courtroom dark suits made him appear more like a stern judge than a sports league major domo. But he fit the mold of the owners of the Original Six franchises, who had agreed to expansion so they could reap the financial rewards of millions in fees for the right to be in the league and to start with a team composed of the unwanted.

Buffalo's and Vancouver's hopes to get respectable soon were based on the amateur draft, the cattle call for the best players at 20 years of age in Canada. (No others were available then, with just a smattering of undrafted Americans in the league. There were no Russians, Swedes, or Czechs.)

Someone on the NHL staff came up with a carnival wheel to settle the selection order. Vancouver would get the single digits up to and including number 9. Buffalo would get 10 to 18. Campbell stepped to the microphone in the smoke-filled ballroom and spun the wheel that sat on a table for all to see.

It slowed to a stop and Campbell called out: "One!" The Vancouver table erupted in cheers. They had won the right to pick Perreault. An assistant whispered to Campbell and pointed to the wheel. The numbers were stacked above each other; it was two number 1s, meaning an 11. "Correction," said Campbell, "the number is 11."

Imlach, the Knoxes, and the table full of Buffalo scouts roared their approval. Imlach put his hand over his heart and smiled. He had been lucky once again, and Gilbert Perreault would be the heart of the franchise for the next 17 seasons. "I was 19 years old," Perreault recalled, "and of course I was nervous, being that I was the first pick overall. I had a lot to prove."

To this day the story goes around that Perreault wore No. 11 in the NHL because of the spin of the wheel, that Imlach asked him to wear it after the Buffalo team came up with the number in the carnival wheel gamble for the first draft choice. "That's not true," Perreault said in December of 2007. "I wore No. 11 my last three years in junior hockey with Montreal, and when I went to camp in Buffalo that's the number I asked for. I don't know if Punch wanted to give it to me anyway, but that's the number I hoped to wear all along."

The Pewter Mug

Another center on that first Buffalo team, Billy Inglis, was no Gilbert Perreault. But he did something no other player could ever claim. He scored the first Buffalo goal in the team's first exhibition game, a 4–4 tie with the New York Rangers on September 17, 1970, in the chilly and damp Peterborough arena. Inglis had been a minor leaguer in the Canadiens organization and was drafted by the Los Angeles Kings in the first NHL expansion in 1967. He played a total of 36 games in the league, 14 with Buffalo late in the first season, with one regular-season goal and three assists. At 5'8" and 157 pounds (soaking wet), Inglis was small, smooth, and the dreaded third "s"—slow. That doomed him to a career in the minors. Ironically, he was nearly as smooth a stickhandler as Perreault, though at three-quarters speed. That night in Peterborough he tapped a rebound past New York's Gilles Villemure to open the Buffalo scoring. The Sabres lurched ahead (it was preseason) by a 4–0 score, but were tied late in the final period by the stronger Rangers.

The Inglis goal is probably only a dim memory to Billy, a soft-spoken cheerful sort who was kind as well as small, not exactly a perfect design for a big-league hockey player. There's just one thing, a mistake that made his goal the object of a collector's passion for all things Sabres. John Boutet, a Grand Island, New York, school teacher, has been assembling Sabres memorabilia since he was a child and now holds a pewter mug that almost went to Inglis at the Sabres' year-end banquet following their first season. The team's management had decided to have mugs engraved with suitable milestones ("first goal," "most goals," "most assists," and so on). The one for Inglis was engraved "First Sabres Goal, Sept. 17, 1971, vs. New York Rangers." A Sabres staffer caught the mistake in time. The date should have been 1970. A new mug was engraved and the mistake ended up in the hands of the club's public relations man, who used it for beer until he passed it on to Boutet for his help in refreshing an aging hockey memory.

Inglis never played much in the NHL, but he later ended up coaching the Sabres in their most tumultuous season of all, when Imlach was fired for defying the ownership.

The Gang That Could Drink Straight

It was widely accepted that professional hockey was fueled by beer in the 1960s and 1970s. General managers and coaches seldom talked about it publicly, but that was largely because they drank the same sudsy stuff when they played. One of the first things a team would settle on in the fall after camp was the location of the postpractice pub in their home city, and they would pass that information on to new team members and rookies. There is a sense of camaraderie that builds among drinkers, hockey players or not. That sense does result in team building as long as the drinking doesn't go too far and turn into drunkenness.

The Boston Bruins of the early 1970s were a swaggering lot, particularly after the team's first Stanley Cup in decades. It didn't hurt that the Bruins had the brilliant Bobby Orr. One year Boston went to training camp in Fitchburg, an old mill town in north central Massachusetts, and worked long and hard at trashing every bar in the city limits. Thirty years later, surviving bartenders and locals still marveled at the Bruins' near-magical ability to make bar stools fly and tables levitate by late afternoon. The initiation rite for Bruins rookies included an informal but effective round of beer swilling that would get both the initiates and the initiators loaded to the gills. Whereupon the flying stool tricks would begin.

It was no different on any other team in professional hockey. The big-leaguers usually gathered in nicer bars and didn't resort to six-pack parties, the drinking mode of choice in the lowest minors, where pay hardly topped double figures a week.

In the early '70s many NHL players still had summer jobs because they needed the money. Two players on the first Buffalo Sabres roster had contracts for $17,500 a year, albeit heavily loaded with performance options that would boost the bucks. However, even in 1970, that wasn't a pay scale on which one could raise a family. So players often had summer jobs, and some of those jobs back in northern Ontario or southern Manitoba were with beer companies.

Players would travel from town to town and hang out with the locals in taverns. Across Canada, the pubs were separate from the dining rooms, and only men were allowed in the pub portions of drinking establishments. Many didn't even have doors on the entrance to men's rooms, which meant drinkers could get to relief points more quickly. An NHL player would walk in the door of the local hotel or tavern and buy a few rounds of the beer he was shilling for the house. This meant happy times for the tavern-keeper and happy customers drinking freely of Molsons, Labatts, or O'Keefe.

A pro hockey player would sometimes come to camp with a beer belly, thanks to his summer job, or thanks to a beer-drinking hobby that began when he was a teenage player humping long bus trips and sneaking from a six-pack while the coach up front pretended not to notice.

Thus were begat the beery Sabres of 1970–71. Punch Imlach's first roster was loaded with NHL veterans who had been made available in the league's expansion draft. It included Phil Goyette from St. Louis, Donnie Marshall from the Rangers, Reggie Fleming from Philadelphia, and Allan Hamilton from New York. Floyd Smith was purchased from Toronto and Dickie Duff was obtained from Los Angeles early in the season. Each had played a decade or more in the league, and without exception they were members of the clan that used beer as a staple beverage, often in place of water. A few of those first Sabres dabbled in the hard stuff, but beer was the staff of life after practice, in the evening, and occasionally into the early morning. Members of the team had gravitated to one downtown Buffalo bar like filings to a magnet. The joint was on a street adjacent to the hotel where Imlach had a suite of his own. It was an old Statler hotel, and its room windows could be opened. Imlach would leave some of them that way on pleasant nights, as downtown traffic was not a noise problem, unlike the cacophony of Manhattan. His players would eventually pay because Punch liked some fresh air.

By the spring of 1971, the Sabres had lost a good chance to make the Stanley Cup playoffs in their first season. That is not to say the team wasn't decent. Perreault and Roger Crozier, the acrobatic and illness-tortured goalie, led the team to what turned out to be the best record of any team outside the playoffs, despite being stuck in a division with five of the original six teams— Montreal, Boston, the Rangers, Detroit, and Toronto.

Come the end of that first season, Imlach had added and subtracted. Many of his original expansion draftees were moved to the minors, and his veterans were running out of gas. He added Eddie Shack from the Los Angeles Kings, a hell-raiser a level above most hell-raisers in the league, who totaled 465 points and 1,437 penalty minutes in his colorful career.

The Musk Ox

Air travel in 1970 was much different for all, even more so for professional athletes. Today's big-leaguers fly in chartered jets, hardly ever mingling with airport crowds or sitting next to a crying baby on a transcontinental flight. In 1970, there seldom were charters, so the Sabres flew with the rest of the citizenry and experienced the same service (or lack thereof) that a regular passenger received. Hockey players in those days tended not to stand out in size the way professional basketball teams or the hulking wide-bodies of pro football did. The first Sabres roster had only three players legitimately over six feet tall (though game program weights and sizes were exaggerated), so they wouldn't

(Left to right) Buffalo mayor Frank Sedita, Sabres owner Seymour Knox, and NHL president Clarence Campbell on Buffalo's opening night, October 15, 1970.

have been that noticeable on a flight with the rest of us, except that they were all young and athletic.

If the Knox brothers had anything to say about it, they would always be recognized when traveling. It all went back to the Knoxes' upbringing. They were both at St. Paul's School in New

Hampshire, one of the most exclusive prep institutions in the country, where every boy wore a school blazer and tie nearly all the time. Seymour and Norty had grown to manhood accustomed to a formality much beyond the average Joe, wearing dark, pin-striped bankers' suits to work, with white shirts and muted ties; perhaps a navy blazer and tie to some casual weekend picnic. They felt their hockey team should look good when traveling and show off its identity with a logo that had been designed just months before.

The original Sabres logo lasted 25 seasons. It was a circle around a silhouetted bison with crossed sabers rampant below. It was conservative; a pictogram that said "buffalo" and "sabers" to a viewer. Or so the Knoxes thought. They outfitted the team with three-brass-button medium blue hopsack blazers with the logo sewn on the breast pocket. The first road trip was for the Sabres first game in the NHL, to face Les Binkley in goal for the Pittsburgh Penguins. On the flight down, all the players wore their blazers, and some even wore the Sabres' club tie, dark blue with tiny logos. The announcers wore dark blue blazers just like the Knoxes. When they all crowded into the aircraft it looked like a prep school reunion.

Imlach didn't much care for the preppy look, but he did demand his players wear a coat and tie while traveling. By the third road trip, however, only a few players wore the blazers, and by the next trip they had disappeared completely. Seymour Knox took after Imlach about the disappearance of the blazers and was told by Imlach: "If you want to be the GM, then you can tell them what to wear." Seymour flushed, but he never brought the subject up again.

It was a good thing. Sabres broadcaster Ted Darling was aboard an Air Canada flight that fall heading west out of Toronto to join the team. He wore his navy blazer with the Sabres crest and was asked by a cabin mate: "What is that thing, a musk ox?" Darling never wore the blazer on the road again.

The Show Opens

The expansion Sabres opened their first season on the road in Pittsburgh, against a mediocre Penguins team. "My first goal... everyone remembers their first goal," said Perreault. "I can't remember the play, but I remember that it was the game winner."

Strangely, Perreault doesn't have that puck today, though his home has plenty of other hockey memories from his 17-season career that ended in selection to the Hockey Hall of Fame.

Jim Watson had a short-lived career as a Buffalo defenseman, but he holds one achievement that can't be challenged. He scored on a long shot against Binkley for the first ever regular-season NHL goal. Buffalo edged the Pens 2–1. The charter flight back to Buffalo that night was a happy one, with the Knoxes and friends aboard. There was no Stanley Cup in sight, but they felt closer to that goal after only one game in the league. The Knoxes were to be bitterly disappointed.

Those Falling Leafs

If there was one game Imlach wanted to win above all others that first season; it was the first against the Toronto Maple Leafs in Maple Leaf Garden. The team's owners, the snide Stafford Smythe and the huffing Harold Ballard, had canned Imlach a year after he coached Toronto to a Stanley Cup in 1967. Punch was bitter about the firing. He had circled that return to Toronto on his desk calendar and reminded the team about it daily.

The bus ride 90 miles up the Queen Elizabeth Way from Buffalo was light on repartee the afternoon of Imlach's "High Noon" game on November 18, 1970. The players dressed more quietly than usual, knowing that any kidding around when Punch was so tense might cause him to send his ever-present hat flying. He was surprised and elated at what happened when the team came out onto Gardens ice. Punch was greeted with a lengthy standing ovation from the 17,000 on hand when he took to the Buffalo bench before the opening faceoff. Now, more than ever,

The "Sabre Girl" Sundae Bafo led Roger Crozier and the team onto the ice on opening night in October 1970.

the game was important to him. "We knew that this game might be as close to a playoff game that we would play all year," recalled Perreault, "so that's the way we tried to play it."

Toronto jumped out to a 2–0 lead, and Imlach stormed back and forth behind the bench in red-faced frustration. Then the floodgates opened. Buffalo scored seven consecutive goals, and an embarrased Stafford Smythe was taunted by a skeptical newspaper reporter who reminded him that Smythe had said there would be no rivalry with Buffalo, because "we'll win every game."

The bus ride back to Buffalo began with smiles of satisfaction, then proceeded to some hoots and hollers after the winning Sabres got into their smuggled six-packs of beer. On every bus ride there are traditional seats; players in the back, media in front of them, and finally the coach and his staff in the first few rows. Imlach liked the right front seat, and he took both seats. Some coaches prefer the one immediately behind the bus driver. But where they sat was as much a part of hockey tradition as the national anthem before the faceoff. And it was an unwritten rule that the coach didn't go down the bus aisle except to visit the rear men's room (if the bus had one). That allowed the players to suck at their beer cans and play poker if it was a long ride. There were other conventions for air travel. Imlach liked to seat his players up front on a commercial flight, perhaps because he heard that tail seats are the most dangerous and the ride the roughest. Later, as all big-league teams began to use charter aircraft almost exclusively, where one sat wasn't as important, but the rigid class structure that gave the coach a certain seat in a certain row (up front) held the way it did on bus rides. I have been aboard several other team charters, and the rules are always the same.

One other thing. On Imlach's buses and airplane charters, no one made a peep for at least a half hour after the Sabres had lost. Imlach needed the time to decompress, as he was an angry loser. When his face faded from crimson to natural, then the players were free to talk above a whisper.

Perreault's Record

With two weeks remaining in the season, the Sabres took on St. Louis at home. The team had overachieved all year, racking up the best point total of all the nonplayoff teams. Buffalo had been in the old East Division, playing the bulk of its schedule against the cream of the Original Six teams, topped by the Canadiens and the Boston Bruins. The crowds in Buffalo's Memorial Auditorium were spotty at first, including a low of about 8,000 souls the night the Sabres played the California Golden Seals despite a promotion that included bringing a live seal onto the ice surface to meet the

Gil Perreault—flanked by Sabres owners Norty (left) and Seymour (right) Knox—is honored by the team.

California team's owner, Charles O. Finley, of baseball fame.

St. Louis was no pushover. The Blues were still strong, though not as strong as when they had dominated after the first NHL expansion in 1967 put them in a division solely made up of expansion clubs. The Blues had reached the Stanley Cup Finals under Scotty Bowman, who combined tight checking and solid goaltending into a model that was better than all the rest of the expansion teams.

In the spring of 1971, there was no Bowman behind the bench, and no Jacques Plante in goal. Yet the Blues were the class of the first wave of expansion teams. Perreault entered that night with a chance to set the rookie goal-scoring record. "Punch was great to me," said Perreault. "He gave me all kinds of ice time all season long. I played the power play, and so I had many chances to get goals."

Perreault was being modest. Imlach played him because Bert was the best he had to play. Even as a rookie, Perreault could make magic on the ice, bobbing and weaving through opponents on end to end rushes. The puck seemed glued to his stick, until that instant he would rifle or feather the perfect pass to his winger or flick a wrist shot past a startled goalie. If there was any criticism of Perreault, it was that he didn't shoot enough. "Punch just told me to go out there and score goals," he said. But Perreault was a playmaker by nature, and his career records prove that.

Late in the third period with the Sabres leading 4–3, Perreault recalls the record-breaking goal: "I was off to the side of the goalie [Ernie Wakely] just outside the crease when Hammy [Al Hamilton] passed me the puck. I just flicked a backhand and there was the goal," he recalled. The usual on-ice love fest followed; his teammates piled on to celebrate. The sellout crowd responded with a roar and a standing ovation. "I think I remember the crowds in Buffalo most," said Perreault. "They were amazing in those early years…just amazing." Perreault's rookie year was but a foreshadowing of the decade ahead, one that would be domination of the league for years by the French Connection.

Chapter 2
Building a Team, Rebuilding an Arena

"When I got to training camp, I knew that if I performed well, I would start on the Sabres… I had 11 goals during the preseason, so that solved that right away."

–Rico Martin

Dave Forman, in a hard hat, supervises raising the roof of the Aud in the summer of 1971—a maneuver that allowed installation of a balcony and nearly 5,000 additional seats.

Raising the Roof

One of the stranger construction jobs in history transformed the Sabres' home arena in the summer of 1971. The franchise had struggled through its first season with a maximum crowd capacity of just over 10,000 seats in Memorial Auditorium. By the second half of the season, nearly every seat was filled most nights, and season-ticket applications for the next year were stacking up like cordwood. The construction job had to happen without any hitches or the Sabres wouldn't have a place to play in the fall.

So what was this critical construction job? It entailed raising the roof of the Aud—literally. Using massive hydraulic jacks, the entire roof of the 32-year-old building would be raised 24 feet to enable construction of a new 4,813-seat balcony. The cheers for Perreault's rookie-record goal had barely faded when workers started knocking through the Aud's exterior walls just under the roof. At an intense pace, they soon had exposed much of the Aud's superstructure near its top. Then jacks were situated on the sidewalks around the elliptical building, used one May morning to raise the roof inch by inch, straining but smooth, powered by massive air compressor machinery. Between dawn and dusk, the roof went up the necessary 24 feet, while rush-hour travelers stared at the building open to the breezes off Lake Erie, an Aud wearing its roof like a precarious top hat. Those Lake Erie breezes air-conditioned the structure for the first time in its history.

Dave Forman was the Sabres' executive vice president and the point man for the team on the construction project. A tinkerer with an expensive collection of cigar-shaped wooden speedboats at his Ontario summer home, Forman was in his glory, checking the job from hour to hour, chatting up construction engineers, and watching the job progress.

"It's the biggest project of this sort that's ever been done," he proudly told me. Using steel and concrete, the contractor built a sloping balcony anchored to the Aud's main vertical steel infrastructure. At first, only canvas tarps hanging over the 24-foot gap around the top of the building protected the inside from the chancy Buffalo weather. By August the gap was closed with concrete blocks all around. The balcony shape was there, hanging at a sharp angle over the Aud's bowl. The principles of geometry required the sharp angle or fans would not have been able to see the entire ice surface from the new balcony seats. The result was a good news–bad news scenario. The good news was that there were no bad seats in the balcony. It was as close to the sides of the rink surface as the seats below, which meant sight lines in the least expensive seats were spectacular compared to the cheapest spots in today's modern facilities, including the HSBC Arena in Buffalo.

The bad news was the steep vertical angle. Walking down the stubby concrete steps to a seat was akin to coming down a mountain trail. Walking back up the steps was a cross between mountain climbing and a stair stepper machine in a fitness center. Some fans who bought season tickets in the new balcony (with seats as low at $3.50 per seat per game) returned them to the Sabres box office after one visit. Fear of heights was a real affliction for those fans.

The view of the game was outstanding. The look from up top slowed the play down, almost like watching a slow-motion replay all the time. Fans could see plays develop, and if they were of an analytical bent, they often preferred the new balcony seats to any other spot in the building.

Next: The Rookies

The Montreal Junior Canadiens were much like their NHL parent team. In the best junior hockey league period—the old Ontario Hockey Association—the junior Habs were successful in developing fast and furious plays and turning out a long line of NHL stars. Even into the first expansion of the NHL in 1967, the Canadiens had first dibs on the best French-Canadian juniors in a sort of ethnic preference the club had wangled from the other owners. Now, under what was called the universal entry draft, clubs took players solely in order of their finish in the standings the year before. The worst picked first. This never seemed to bother the Canadiens organization. General manager Sam Pollock was adept at trading off his second-line players to poor NHL teams where the Montreal castoffs were still better than what was on the poor teams' rosters. In return, Pollock maneuvered first-round picks in the draft.

Thus in June 1971, Pollock was at a Queen Elizabeth Hotel table softly talking into the table microphone to select Guy Lafleur of the Quebec Ramparts as the first draft choice overall. Montreal had not been able to stash players with the Junior Canadiens as they were allowed to do in the past, so Lafleur had played to the east in Quebec City. Lafleur was a franchise player whose swooping skating style—long-legged with a mane of dark blond hair waving—brought the Montreal Forum crowd to its feet for more than a decade.

The first Montreal Junior Canadien drafted was the fifth overall pick, a pick that belonged to Buffalo. Imlach spoke as softly as Pollock into his table's microphone. "Buffalo selects Ree-chard Mar-tan," Imlach said, stressing his version of French pronunciation. Richard Martin was a left winger who had led the OHA in goal-scoring the winter before with 71. His team had won the Memorial Cup (Canada's junior hockey championship), and he was a first-team All-Star. Martin was considered a "natural goal scorer," a term applied by coaches to someone who has both the knack and the shot to back it up. Martin's forte was his slap shot, one of the hardest in the game, released quickly because he only used a short back swing. His wrist shot was as hard as some players' slappers, and he could shoot it hard in stride or off stride.

Though he was French-Canadian, Martin was equally at home speaking English, and he spoke with no French accent. He had played with Perreault in junior, though not on the same line, so Imlach had plans to team him up with Bert from the moment he was drafted.

"When I got to training camp, I knew that if I performed well, I would start on the Sabres," he recalled. "I had 11 goals during the preseason schedule, so that solved that right away. My center was Phil Goyette in camp, and I wore No. 8. Punch called me in just before the season started and told me Gilbert [Perreault] was going to be my center. Bert had come to camp about 25 pounds over his playing weight, and Imlach said he was pairing me with him because I could skate him into shape."

"You're the only one who can skate with him," Martin was told by Imlach. "Make him skate. Make him skate."

In Buffalo's second round, Imlach chose a Peterborough player, another left winger who hadn't been a big scorer in junior but who would turn into one of the best checkers in the league for nearly a decade and a half. Craig Ramsay, like Martin, didn't have the luxury of learning his pro craft in the minor leagues. Imlach needed help in Buffalo fast, and he decided to infuse his expansion team with youth in that second season in the hope his "kids" would develop. His third-round pick was a gangling defenseman from western Canada named Bill Hajt. That trio of rookies was the best single draft, it would turn out, in the team's history.

"I was a Montreal kid," recalled Martin. "So on draft day, I just had to drive to the meeting and hear my name chosen fifth overall. It was a thrill, of course, but I didn't know quite what to expect. Punch talked with me and told me that he expected I would start right away in the NHL, unless I had a bad training camp. He introduced me to the Knoxes, who invited me to come up and visit Buffalo over the summer and 'bring your sticks.' They knew that I was a serious golfer, and when I came for that visit we played Crag Burn [golf course]."

Martin was the flashy new story in the Sabres' second season. With his good looks and better hockey talent, Martin began an NHL career that was star-crossed, but seemed in the beginning to steer him toward the Hockey Hall of Fame. His center and power play mate, Perreault, had set the rookie goal record the year before. Martin was taken in the same draft as Lafleur and Marcel Dionne, both Hall of Famers after their career, but as a rookie, it was Martin who went on a goal-scoring rampage. Late in the season he potted number 39 in Toronto against an aging Jacques Plante, and by the end of the year he had 44 in all.

A free spirit then, and a free spirit now, Martin explained how he scored the record 39th. "I got a pass from Al Hamilton [who also assisted on Perreault's record 38th] and just whirled around and let a wrist shot go. Setting a record in Toronto was nice, especially because Imlach liked to beat Toronto more than anyone else."

Martin could skate as fast as Perreault, but Perreault was the literal center of play when he was on the ice. It was notable that in large measure, Gilbert's skills as a playmaker kept opposing defensemen so busy that his wingers benefited, including the brash Martin.

Rico was one of the first rookies in Buffalo—but certainly not the last—who was impressed by the fervor of the fans on the Niagara Frontier. "The biggest thing is, coming from Montreal, I was used to playing in front of large crowds. We actually outdrew the [NHL] Montreal Canadiens. I was used to a lot of attention, but nothing like what I received when I was with the Sabres. Buffalo was a lot smaller than Montreal, so no matter where you went people knew who you were. It was exciting. You just couldn't get away from the game if you tried. No matter where you went you were recognized, so in essence you were always kind of on your best behavior.

"The people were absolutely ecstatic about getting a new hockey team that was exciting and that was doing so well. They were great years, those first five years leading to when we went to the [Stanley] Cup. It was fun to be a part of it."

Martin's reputation for a blazing slap shot and the speed to skate with Perreault allowed him to make his hockey mark as a rookie. "There's a time for fun, and a time to be serious," he recalled. "If you can't have fun, then life isn't very much, is it?"

Over time Richard became "Rico" to his friends and team-mates. He was the bane of his team's existence off the ice, constantly pulling pranks on them. "I wasn't the only one," he said. "Schony [Jim Schoenfeld] and [Jerry] Korab were as bad as I was," he insisted.

Ramsay Finds a Line

Craig Ramsay is currently a successful NHL coach who generally works to instruct the nuances of defensive play. When he came up to the Sabres early in the 1971–72 season, Ramsay was a lockup defensive winger in search of line mates who could play the same way, and then some.

Don Luce had been obtained from the Detroit Red Wings. Given a chance to play regularly by Imlach, he thrived with Ramsay on his left side. Together the pair became the best penalty killers in the league for more than a decade. Imlach had to be crafty if he was going to improve the expansion Sabres quickly. The draft was one answer, but not *the* answer, as it would take too long to develop a 20-man winning team from the annual selection process. Yet he had little to trade, except people like Perreault, Martin, and Ramsay, and they weren't about to be traded. Punch managed to trade for a little bit of improvement at a time.

"If I can improve my team just 5 percent with a trade," he said, "then I will. Some of the trades don't seem to be much to a fan, but if I think they help a little bit, I'll make them. After a few 'small' deals, we may be looking at a team that's 20 percent better, and that may mean the playoffs."

By the third season Imlach's juggling, trading, and drafting paid off in the tough Eastern Division, populated by five of the Original Six teams. Buffalo had to beat out one to make the Stanley Cup playoffs, and the Sabres did it the last night of the season, edging Detroit.

"The first year we made the playoffs was wonderful," recalled Ramsay. "We had to win the last game against St. Louis and we did it, 3–1. Then we went on to play Montreal in the old Forum, and I scored the first Sabres playoff goal, though we lost 2–1. It was super to play Montreal in the Forum. We won Game 5 in overtime when Rene Robert scored. We lost the series in six [games] at home, but it was pretty neat to play Montreal. The Canadiens were really good and they, of course, went on to win the Stanley Cup in that spring of 1973."

The French Connection

By the spring of 1972, Eddie Shack had worn out his hockey welcome in Buffalo. He was a character at a time when Imlach needed characters to distract the fans while his younger players matured, but that time had ended. Shackie was near the end of his career in the NHL, and the hell-bent-for-leather skating style that was his trademark had fallen a stride behind the play. Meanwhile, the Pittsburgh Penguins were willing to trade right winger Rene Robert.

Imlach had selected Robert in what was called the intraleague draft in the previous summer, but Pittsburgh had

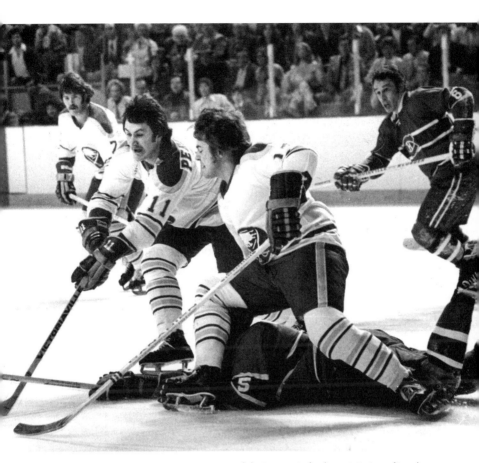

The French connection in flight: Martin (7), Perreault (11), and Robert (front).

scooped him back from the Buffalo roster in its drafting turn. The arcane proceedings of the intraleague draft have long disappeared from the league, to the good fortune of the fans and media that had tried to figure out the whole bureaucratic mess.

Robert had come up through the Toronto organization under Imlach's reign there, and Punch felt he could become a scorer in the NHL with the right opportunity. In Buffalo Rene got just that. Punch immediately put him on the line with Martin and Perreault. Their speed alone made the line a force to be reckoned with. In the final 12 games of the schedule, a rejuvenated Robert scored nine goals.

Martin explained how the line was named after a popular crime-chase movie of that year, one that starred Gene Hackman as "Popeye" Doyle, one of the great tough cop roles in the American cinema.

"A Buffalo newspaperman named Lee Coppola used to work part-time writing messages on the light boards that hung on the balcony faces in Memorial Aud," said Martin. "Late in the season, I looked up after a goal we scored as a line, and there he had written something like, 'Rick from Bert and Rene.... It's a French Connection.' Actually I don't remember which of us scored that goal, but from that night on, we were the French Connection."

Today Martin is a successful computer industry executive still living in the Buffalo area, happy to be known as part of one of hockey's most famous line combinations. "I get introduced as 'Rick Martin, the old hockey player,'" he recalled. "Then someone invariably says, 'Who?' 'You know…from the French Connection.' Then everyone knows who I am."

Several years ago the Sabres organization inducted Martin, Perreault, and Robert into the Sabres Hall of Fame on the same night, and a French Connection banner hangs from the rafters at HSBC Arena to this day. As for Lee Coppola, who tagged them with the nickname? He hasn't made a dime off it, and some question whether it even happened that way.

An Agent Is Rebuffed

Imlach may have liked Martin as a hockey player, but he had a different attitude toward Martin's agent, a Montreal lawyer named Larry Sazant. The Sabres were still in their first suite of offices, near Buffalo's City Hall, on the second floor of a building that housed one of the region's prominent law firms. There were stairs, but they were hard to spot when you walked into the building foyer, so nearly everyone took a small and slow elevator when visiting the team's offices. Outside the elevator on the second floor was an area too small to be a foyer, just a linoleum floor and plain walls. It was a bit claustrophobic.

Sazant arrived with attaché case in hand one sunny afternoon primed and ready to make a good deal for his client, who, after all, was the fifth pick among the best juniors in North America. The trouble was that Imlach didn't like to deal with agents at all. "I only pay a player a certain amount, a number I determine in his value to the team," he told the author on several occasions. "If they get an agent, they don't get any more money from me. They're just giving some of it away." Imlach's Scottish roots and personality didn't allow him to spend more money than necessary on any hockey player. When Punch decided to be obdurate, he was as stubborn a man as there was in the NHL.

So when Sazant arrived and asked to see Punch, he was informed he would have to wait for a while. He was directed back outside the offices to a seat in a hard-back chair next to the elevator. There he sat for several hours, composure intact (though that's difficult to understand) and played a waiting game with Imlach. Most who got off the elevator were taken aback by the man in the dark suit who sat and waited…and waited…and waited. Imlach arranged for others to visit his office that afternoon and had his secretary wave them in while Martin's agent sat. Punch's instructions were that no one was to offer Sazant a coffee or a soft drink. He finally let the agent into his office after the place was closed for the day.

In these days of multimillion-dollar contracts and multimillion-dollar agents, a GM like Punch wouldn't get a job, or hold it, if he acted that way. But when the NHL teams held the whip hand, agents were to be humbled at every turn, at least in the world of Imlach.

Down on the Farm

One of the first requirements of an NHL franchise is to have a farm team in the high minor leagues. When Imlach took on the Sabres, he also had to find a place for his rookies and his prospects to play if they couldn't reach the Buffalo roster. In 1970 he stashed players under a working agreement with the Salt Lake City Golden Eagles of the Western Hockey League. Salt Lake was owned and operated by Dan Meyer, whose regular business was mining and mine stock speculation. At the time, Buffalo would have liked to place its players on a team closer to Buffalo, as the distance and time required to bring in a guy from Salt Lake was at least a day. There weren't then—and aren't now—any direct flights to Buffalo from the Utah city. Then again, all of Buffalo's best young players (which amounted to Perreault) were on the varsity in Buffalo.

By the spring of 1971, Imlach itched for a team in the American Hockey League, whose teams were located in the eastern third of the country. Usually when Imlach itched, the Knox brothers came up with the scratch. After talking to the AHL about a franchise in Florida (read: retired Canadians as possible fans) they bought a lower minor league franchise in Cincinnati and applied for a franchise in the league. Owning one's own minor league franchise was the thing to do, at least as far as Punch was concerned. He felt he could control the coaching and player development more closely that way. Punch convinced his old friend and minor league business partner, Joe Crozier, to coach the team in Cincy.

One of the players slated for Cincinnati was Bill Hajt, a lanky 6'3" 200-pounder from the small farm town of Radisson, Saskatchewan. "I went to that first training camp, and I was just a kid. I got homesick," Hajt recalled. So he left camp. "Maybe I wasn't grown up enough, being from a small town in western Canada. I was still trying to seek my own identity and what I was going to do in life. Maybe it was the best thing that happened to me. Jean [his longtime girlfriend] and I got married. That year away [from the sport] made me realize how much I really loved hockey. I had been playing organized hockey since I was four years old. I did some soul searching and realized that I had a chance to maybe play in the NHL or at least a high level of organized hockey, so I decided to try it again the next fall."

It was a good thing for the Sabres. Hajt played two seasons in Cincinnati and was promoted to Buffalo in 1974. He played 14 seasons in a Sabres uniform and was an All-Star Game selection in 1981.

Principle and $500

Left winger Craig Ramsay was the Sabres' second-round draft choice in 1971. He had played his junior hockey in Peterborough with the OHA "Petes," under Coach Roger Neilson, who later would become the coach of the Sabres. In the early 1970s a second-round draft choice—for that matter, any round draft choice—didn't have much leverage in contract negotiations. Draftees were just beginning to hire agents to represent them, but the money wasn't more than chump change compared to today.

Ramsay recalled his *modus operandi* becoming a professional hockey player: "I didn't have a car when I was drafted. I had not signed my contract, so I actually took a bus from Peterborough to Toronto where I met my agents and they drove me to St. Catharines. That was the first time I ever saw a professional hockey contract. I didn't like it much. I got to the hotel and John Andersen [the Sabres director of scouting] came and asked me if I had signed my contract. I told them I wasn't going to sign it. That started a three-day process of negotiations between John and myself. Back and forth, we would talk. Then he would go and talk to Punch because Punch wouldn't talk to me. Imlach finally put an extra $500 in one year and an extra $1,000 in another year. I agreed after three days after a couple of minor adjustments to sign the contract. I had been going through training camp already without a contract. Holding out for three days got me an extra 500 bucks. It doesn't seem like much, but it was the principle."

The Rookie Ride

Ramsay's training camp was different from what rookies experience today. The twin rinks in St. Catharines were full of hockey players all day long. Ramsay recalled the experience: "We practiced twice a day, a couple of hours each time. There were a lot of bodies there, players for Salt Lake, for Cincinnati, for Charlotte, and of course for Buffalo. It was a pretty intimidating time. Reggie Fleming gave me my real introduction [to pro hockey] when he just flattened me in a scrimmage and then skated over and said: 'Rookie, keep your head up.' It was a pretty interesting time to break in. I had already played junior against Gilbert Perreault and I knew how good he was; a dominant player. I had played against Richard Martin also. But that was about it in players I knew.

"We played our last exhibition game in Peterborough, and from there I went up on a bus to Toronto with Joe Crozier [the Cincinnati coach that fall] and Angie Nigro [the trainer]. We flew into Cincinnati and the next day they had a little motorcade parade in convertibles through the streets of Cincinnati. No one knew us and no one seemed to really care. They didn't know what we were doing. It was great, riding in the back of an open convertible waving to people who didn't know or care who we were.

"I played 19 games there. Then one night we were playing in Baltimore when Joe Crozier called me in and said, 'Play good tonight, kid, because I'm sending you up [to the Sabres] after the game.' I didn't play very well. We lost, 4–0, and looked like a pretty bad team. But I was sent up anyway.

"I flew to Buffalo and took a cab downtown. There was nobody there to meet me. I made my way to the rink [Memorial Auditorium] where I met one of the trainers, and he told me to come back at 5:00 PM, that the game was at 7:00 PM. I played that night against the Toronto Maple Leafs."

A Rookie Gets a Sticky Welcome

Another rookie draftee that season played two years in Cincinnati before climbing into the Sabres' back line. Hajt remembers when he came of age against the Bruins in Memorial Auditorium: "It was one of the first games we played that season in Buffalo. I was kind of a young kid—23—and Wayne Cashman came into the corner, so I took a little run at him. After he went into the boards, I was skating back up the ice, when out of the blue from behind me, I feel a little tug on the corner of my mouth.

Getty Images

Craig Ramsay was a lock-down defensive player for the Sabres.

It was his hockey stick. He had turned it around as a weapon and it stuck in the corner of my mouth. He didn't pull it, but it was if he was saying, 'Hey, rookie, if you hit me, this is what's going to happen to you.'

"How simple he could have done it. Nobody would have seen it and he could have split me wide open. It was a signal from an old veteran to this kid to cool it. It scared the hell out of me at the time."

"Let's Get the Hell Out of Here."

Hajt reprised one of his most unusual moments on the ice: "We were playing in Montreal. At that time most of us didn't wear helmets, so we were always conscious of guys who shot high. It was the second period. They're in our end and the puck scrambles around the boards and out to the point to John Van Boxmeer. I'm in front of the net with Peter Mahovlich [of the Canadiens], and we're jostling. He wants to screen the goalie, and I'm trying to get him out of the way.

"John had a reputation for shooting the puck at [what looked like] 3,000 miles an hour. And he always shot it high. I had the same reputation about high, hard shots. Peter looked at me, and I looked at him, because we both saw who was winding up to shoot. It was a one-timer. He wasn't even going to stop to tee it up. So we knew Boxy was going to be totally out of control. Peter grabbed me by the scruff of the neck, and he said: 'Bill, let's get the "f" out of here.' He pulled me right into the corner. He didn't want to look bad by getting out of the way. When he pulled me, I moved. Peter was a big guy, so when he wanted you to go somewhere, you didn't have a choice. We no sooner got out of the way and Boxy fires it head high, right over the top of the net. It went all the way around the glass and down to the opposite end of the rink. I turned to Mahovlich and said, 'Thanks, Peter.' Then we both skated out of the zone as if nothing had happened. I never had anything like that happen in my hockey life."

Chapter 3
"All Like Dogs..."

*"When a fight would break out...
[Tim] Horton didn't bother with
punches most times. He would just
grab his opponent in a bear hug and
that would be the end of the scrap."*

–Paul Wieland

Getty Images

Defenseman Tim Horton, a member of the Hockey Hall of Fame best known for many great years in Toronto, was killed in a car accident during his second season with the Sabres.

The Comeback

In the late summer of 1972 Imlach had his eyes on another defenseman. Tim Horton was a star for more than a decade in Toronto, including holding the anchor position on Imlach's 1967 Stanley Cup team. He had finally moved out of Maple Leafs blue and into that of the Broadway Blues—the New York Rangers. But after a brief stop in New York, he had spent part of a season with Pittsburgh and then decided to retire. Nonetheless Imlach had selected Horton in the intraleague draft and spent weeks trying to coax the six-time All-Star into playing again, this time in Buffalo blue and gold. During the first week of the regular season Punch had his man. Horton had already started the chain of donut shops that bears his name, but five big zeros following a one brought him out of retirement, at a salary estimated at $100,000 for the season. That was big-time money, near the top of the league in 1972.

Horton had missed training camp, though he was hardly out of shape. Still considered by many as the strongest man ever to play in the NHL, Tim walked into the Memorial Aud dressing room and laced on skates late one afternoon. He sat patiently on a straight-back chair before taking the ice alone, then answered a barrage of questions from the Buffalo media. After Tim had explained he was returning because he loved the game, a reporter asked him about Imlach. It was a loaded question, as Punch was known for being truculent at best in his coaching methods, and even angrier when things didn't go right. "How does Punch treat you guys?" was the question. Horton smiled and hit the batting practice fastball kind of question. "That's easy," he said. "He treats us all the same...like dogs."

The Strongest Man in Hockey?

Tim Horton was strong, that was for sure. When a fight would break out on the ice, woe the dummy who tried to take him on. Horton didn't bother with punches most times. He would just grab his opponent in a bear hug and that would be the end of the scrap. Horton could hug so hard that it was nearly impossible to break his grip.

His strength came into play on one occasion in the donut business, of all places. A writer from a Toronto newspaper and I witnessed Horton on the location site of a new Tim Horton's donut store in Fort Erie, Ontario, opposite Buffalo across the Peace Bridge. We had tagged along to watch Horton ("Horty" to his teammates and friends) deal with the delivery of the structural steel for the store's frame. The reporter thought the difference between Horton the hockey player and Horton the donut entrepreneur would make for an interesting piece.

We arrived and waited only a few minutes when there appeared a large tractor-trailer with steel pieces and rods stacked aboard. A crew of four had been hired to unload, but for some reason, they didn't show up on time. Horty was impatient that afternoon, as he had another appointment later on. He was dressed for business, wearing a tan suit with a vest and a blue shirt and darker blue tie. His pectoral muscles bulged through the expensive tailoring. There was no way they could hide. Horton conferred with the truck driver and pulled out his wallet. Then he took off the suit coat and vest and rolled up his sleeves.

Tim and the driver, with Tim doing most of the bull work, yanked pieces off the trailer bed and slid them to the ground. They carried the steel and stacked it neatly on the store's cleared land site. It took them a good 90 minutes, as we waited to no avail for the four helpers to arrive. When it was over, Horton hardly looked like he had broken a sweat, though it was a balmy April day. He rolled down his cuffs, put his vest and suit coat back on, and pulled his tie knot up.

"Good day, gentlemen," he said as he drove off to make the appointment. We got tired just watching him work.

The Donut King

His donuts were called Tim Horton's Donuts when the first of the company's locations opened in southern Ontario in 1969. Today, 34 years after Horton's death, the company has changed not only its ownership but also its very name, in a very subtle way. The chain of Horton donut locations is now the most famous Canadian brand in Canada, with 2,300 stores (most franchised) located literally from sea to sea, dotting nearly all the places where people congregate in Canada. There are several hundred stores in the United States, largely located near the Canada-U.S. border. Buffalo has dozens in the metropolitan area, but Rochester, just 60 miles down the road, doesn't have any.

We're talking here about Horton the hockey player adding his name to a donut chain that would first make it on the strength of his All-Star eminence in hockey and a decade and a half with the Maple Leafs. His was a name familiar to millions of Canadians who never saw him play, those millions that made listening to Foster Hewitt on Saturday night's *Hockey Night in Canada* a common cultural experience and part of Canada's heritage.

Today, few Horton locations even have a picture of Tim as a Leafs, Rangers, and Sabres player on the wall anymore. Even fewer of the young employees know who he was or what he did for a living. A story in the Toronto *Globe and Mail* in 2005 reported how Horton had nearly vanished from the chain that bears his name.

But the company's name has changed in a subtle way because of the province of Quebec's language sign laws. In that French-speaking part of Canada, all signs on businesses must be in French. Hence, a few years back Tim Horton's (the possessive) became Tim Hortons (the plural) in the French-speaking province. A company spokesperson said it was easier to change the signs all across the chain to conform to the Quebec version than to have every bit of signage, letterhead, and so forth, to be different in most of Canada from the name in French.

Maybe it's fitting that even Horton's ghost couldn't claim ownership today.

The Plunge

In January 1972, NHL coaches, general managers, owners, and other team and league officials were at a Minneapolis hotel, the headquarters for the midseason All-Star Game festivities. When the NHL meets, the hotel lobby is abuzz with hockey gossip, as the media circulate through the crowd, looking for inside information about trades and firings. That afternoon the Radisson lobby was no exception, the glass-roofed atrium noisy and the bar crowded with the men of the NHL, an hour before the All-Star banquet in the hotel ballroom was to begin.

Suddenly there was a loud boom above the crowd. It sounded as if someone had dropped a bomb on the shatterproof glass ceiling. A different buzz went through the crowd, briefly concerned with what happened to cause the noise. A dozen floors above them, a few people knew what happened. They included Bobby Hull of the Blackhawks and Paul Henderson of the Maple Leafs, who a few moments before were on their way to their rooms to change clothes for the banquet when they passed an open room door, with the bitter winter wind howling into the hallway. Hull and Henderson looked inside to see someone hanging onto the window ledge at the other end. They called out, but the man hanging let go and plunged to the atrium glass roof below. The players were shaken and ran into the hallway to call authorities. In the hall, they ran into Dave Forman of the Sabres, who was on his way to his room. Hull and Henderson were aghast. "Someone just jumped," Hull said in a shaken voice. Forman moved into the empty wind-blown room and picked up the phone to call the front desk.

He then hung up and called the switchboard to ask for the room of Dan Meyer, the owner of the Salt Lake City Golden Eagles, the former Sabres farm club, who was to sit with Forman at the banquet. The switchboard operator told Forman, "You're on the phone in that room, sir."

"I stood there for a second or two trying to process what she had said to me," Forman recalled. "Then I realized that Dan must have been the guy who jumped. I can't ever remember being so shocked."

According to press reports the next few days, Dan Meyer had received news that his financial interests in a mining venture had been lost in the volatile market, and that he was broke. That, it appeared, was the reason for his suicide.

Seymour's Wallet

The Knox brothers were part of a western New York family that traced many of its millions to the Woolworth stores. They had been raised with servants around at all times, and they had gone the proper educational route of the very rich: a New England prep school and four years at an Ivy League college, in their case, Yale University. They were very much gentlemen, except when Norty became angry. Then the younger brother would let off steam in a most ungentlemanly way. By and large, Seymour and Norty were pleasant people to work for and were admired by most of their staff and the players who came in contact with them.

Like many of their peers, the brothers operated in a world of wealth, but not a world of money. Nearly everything they did was in that wealthy environment, where merely being who you are means your bill is sent at the end of the month, your secretary makes all the plane and hotel reservations, and you never shop for groceries or just about anything else. That's done by the hired help. In the early 1970s credit cards weren't as common as they are today, and therein lies the tale.

Norty Knox had decided on the name of the new Sabres minor league franchise in Cincinnati, passing on Cossacks to call the team the Swords. In August of 1971, the brothers had scheduled a news conference in a Cincinnati hotel to formally announce the team and unveil its uniform (exactly like the parent Sabres but with crossed swords beneath a capital *C*).

That meant a plane trip to the Ohio city with me. I was the Sabres public relations director at the time and had been instructed to do the same job for the new team, at least for this media event. Said event went off well, with newspapermen, a columnist or two, and cameras from local television stations on hand. After a cab ride to the airport for the return trip to Buffalo, the Knoxes and I headed for the bar with a two-hour wait ahead for our flight. Barely seated at a table, Seymour Knox told me to "charge the drinks to your expense account." I was surprised, since it was his money in the end no matter what, but I went to the bar and returned with our beverages of choice. "You know why my brother asked you to charge the drinks to expenses, don't you?" Norty asked. His answer to his question: "Because he doesn't have any money; he never has any money in his wallet."

Seymour flushed and retorted: "I do too, Norty. It's just that it's easier for Paul to pay." Norty smiled and challenged Seymour. "Come on, get out your wallet and let's see. I'll bet you don't have more that five bucks in there." Seymour pulled out his wallet and we looked inside. Norty Knox was wrong. There were only two lonely singles inside. One of upstate New York's richest men traveled with not enough money to buy a Happy Meal. *Noblesse oblige* was a Knox strong suit.

Chapter 4
Take Another Step

"I was absolutely delighted to have been traded to Buffalo…. We had a group of young players who were pretty raw around the edges, but there was some enormous talent there."

—Jim Lorentz

The Buildup

There were no high-priced free agents in the NHL during the 1970s. A free agent was someone who couldn't get a contract as a pro hockey player. There were only two ways to improve a roster: through trades and through the draft of amateur players. The draft was less of a crap shoot than it is today, as the stock of players available was confined to North America, more specifically to Canada. Nearly every NHL player came up through the junior hockey programs across Canada, with the Ontario Hockey League usually getting the best juniors.

Until the NHL expanded in 1967, most junior "A" (the top tier) teams were owned by an NHL club. Juniors in the past had been a form of involuntary servitude from the age of 14 or so when players signed what was known as a "C Form." That was the piece of paper tying the player to a specific NHL organization—let's say the Boston Bruins—until release or 'death do they part'. In return, the player was vetted through the Bruins organization and, if good enough, placed on the roster of one of Boston's top junior clubs. In the 1968 Memorial Cup, the series for Canada's Junior Hockey title, the Bruins Estevan team, called—interestingly—the Bruins, played against Boston's OHA junior club, the Niagara Falls Flyers. All the games but the second (which was played in Montreal's Forum) were played in the home arena of the Flyers.

Niagara Falls was led by Derek Sanderson, later a Boston star, and both rosters were filled with talent that went on to NHL careers. The Flyers won easily in five games, including four overtimes in the fourth contest.

That was the point. Junior hockey was the NHL's amateur farm system, and some teams were more successful than others at stocking talent. There was no secret formula. Just find the best kids as young as possible, and lock them up for their career. NHL teams had dozens of "bird dog" scouts to comb the country for the best kids at age 14. The age factor at the other end also made spotting talent less than the lottery it is today. Juniors were not eligible for NHL draft until they were turning 20. Two more years of junior play usually separated the wheat from the chaff in NHL potential. Juniors were in some cases allowed to play an extra year to age 21, but few of those players ever made the pros.

With the first expansion, there was a gradual move toward a draft of all players, but it didn't happen until 1970, as the original six teams claimed they needed three years to move their "C Form" players through their amateur team systems.

Buffalo was the first team to select in 1970 in what was called the universal amateur draft. The Sabres selected Perreault. This new draft meant all junior players, and later foreign players and college players, were subject to selection based on the reverse order of finish in the NHL standings the year before. The draft couldn't supply all the answers in Buffalo during the first three seasons of Imlach's reign as GM. He would need some of the luck that Punch always said he had in abundance.

Rico

While he excelled at creating mayhem on the ice with his heavy shot and lightning speed, Rico Martin's penchant for playing pranks almost cost Buffalo a game against the Montreal Canadiens. He explained: "Rick Dudley was very intense, and he didn't pay close attention to his equipment like most of us. So he was a perfect mark for a trick that we liked to play. You might remember that sticks were wooden back then, and the shaft and blade came together where the bend is. Stick manufacturers used to put a piece of tape around that joint, with alternating colored stripes. My trick was to take the tape off carefully, then saw through the joint about halfway, put the tape back on, and when a guy took a slap shot in practice or in warm-up, the stick would break and he'd fall on his face while the rest of us laughed.

"I fixed up three of Rick Dudley's sticks that way one day with Montreal in town for a game that evening. As it happened, Rick picked up those three sticks and took them out for the pregame warm-up. So help me, he didn't take a single slap shot in the warm-up—all wristers—so not a stick broke. He left them on the bench stick rack for use as game sticks. Frankly, I had forgotten all about it in the rush of getting ready to face the Canadiens, so when Rick got a breakaway late in the second period, I was as surprised as anyone when he took a slap shot 15 feet in front of the goalie. The stick broke and he nearly fell on his face. No goal, of course.

"A linesman brought the broken stick to our bench and one of the trainers—Angie Nigro—looked it over. 'What the hell' or something like that, he yelled. I sat there on the bench looking straight ahead. We played a great third period—we had to—and fortunately won the game. Can you imagine what a coach would say if he found out we lost a game because of a gag gone wrong? I got rid of the other sticks that had been sawed as soon as I could."

Enter Lorenzo

In the midst of the 1971–72 season Punch Imlach continued his practice of making small improvements to the Sabres lineup in keeping with his bit-by-bit theory of improvement. One of those bits was a player who bit off more than anyone first thought he could chew. Jim Lorentz had been an outstanding junior with the Niagara Falls Flyers of the OHA. The Waterloo, Ontario, native was a center of the old school, deft at puck handling, somewhat slight of build for a big-leaguer by today's standards, and not the fastest skater. Yet he turned out to be what coaches call a "gamer," a player who made his skills work for him because of determination and hockey intelligence.

As a junior he was property of the Boston Bruins and had come up to the NHL through their farm system, arriving in the Hub for a first full season in the fall of 1969. That season the Bruins won the Stanley Cup with the likes of Bobby Orr, Gerry Cheevers, and Wayne Cashman in their lineup. Lorentz—who soon had the nickname "Lorenzo"—was a fourth-line player on the Bruins, but he had a Cup to sip from in his first full year in the NHL.

The next season he found himself in St. Louis, where he was given more ice time and responded with 19 goals and 21 assists, a solid total for a young player, stats that would have seemed to promise an even bigger role for the Blues in 1971–72. But for some reason, things didn't click from the beginning that fall of 1971, and Lorenzo was shipped off to the New York Rangers, where Emile "the Cat" Francis was the GM. Francis was a genial and garrulous ex-goalie who was liked by most of his players. Lorentz didn't play much in New York either.

Lorentz described the night he came to Buffalo to stay: "I was absolutely delighted to have been traded to Buffalo. I really liked Francis. He was very honest and upfront with me. He promised me that if they weren't going to play me on a regular basis that he would trade me.

"We were on a road trip and were playing the Sabres in Buffalo that night. During the second intermission—I was not dressed for that game—he called me into the dressing room. In those days in the Aud there was another room off the main dressing room for the visitors. He sat me down and said I'd been traded to the Sabres. I was ecstatic because I'd played junior hockey with the Niagara Falls Flyers. It was close to home. I had so many friends in the area. He wished me luck and left the room to address the Rangers team in the main dressing room. In the meantime I was by myself in the room, and I went to the bathroom.

"The Rangers trainer looked in the room, didn't see anybody, so shut and locked the door. So there I was traded to the Buffalo Sabres. I wanted to call people and tell them, but I couldn't get out of the room because it was locked. I was pounding on the door, no luck. I spent the whole period locked in the room. Finally at the end of the game they opened the room and there I was. I was delighted to be traded to Buffalo. I knew I was going to get a fair opportunity to play because at that time they weren't a very good team."

That was Lorenzo's first impression. But he soon realized that the talent level was improving quickly in Buffalo. "We had a group of young players who were pretty raw around the edges," he recalled, "but there was some enormous talent there—Gilbert Perreault, Richard Martin, and later that year, Rene Robert. Punch and the organization were making some terrific moves and at the same time they had great drafts—guys like Jim Schoenfeld and later Danny Gare.

"You could see that given a few years, this was going to be a very good team. It was one of those situations where all these players came together and there was instant chemistry. They methodically built an outstanding team that really got along well together. That to me was one of the keys, having played in Boston on the 1970 Stanley Cup team. *Chemistry*, a word we hear all the time in pro sports, but it's enormously important. You can have great talent, put it together, and it just doesn't jell. Our team jelled. We had a little bit of everything. We had a bit of toughness, talent, and we had hardworking guys who played hard for each other."

In a smaller NHL, players saw each other on the ice more often. Rivalries were often fierce, and it wasn't that unusual that teams would play each other back-to-back games. Of course, compared to the times of the Original Six, when teams played each other 14 times a season and then again in the playoffs, there weren't quite as many intense games. The Sabres and Vancouver had expanded the league to 14 teams. There was an unbalanced schedule, with the result that Lorentz would not play often against St. Louis during the 1972–73 season. But the Blues were in town on the final night of the regular schedule, and a Buffalo win would push aside Detroit and put the Sabres in the Stanley Cup playoffs for the first time in their three-year history.

It was Lorenzo's first big moment—but certainly not his last—as a Sabre. "I scored late in the third period. Gerry Meehan set me up from behind the net, and that was the goal—in terms of cementing a playoff position. It was a very exciting time," he recalled.

Luce on the L-o-o-s-e

Things sometimes worked out in the old NHL. Players who were selected the first few seasons after the draft came into the game were often slotted by their drafting teams into roles that were predetermined. When Don Luce was chosen by the New York Rangers in the third round (14th overall), he was coming into

Don Luce and Jim Schoenfeld enjoy a charter-flight card game.

pro hockey as a playmaker and scorer in junior hockey. Luce had piled up 94 points with the Kitchener Rangers in his final junior season, and the Rangers expected he could do the same as a pro.

Luce spent nearly two seasons with New York's Central League farm club in Omaha, Nebraska, before a call-up late in the

1969–70 season. At Omaha that year, he was named the first-team All-Star center in year-end balloting. He played 12 games in the NHL and then five more in the playoffs. He hadn't yet blossomed into a big pro scorer, so the Rangers moved him to Detroit early in the fall of 1970. In limited ice time with Detroit, Luce still didn't score, and thus was available the next May to Imlach in Buffalo. Punch sent goalie Joe Daley to the Red Wings for Luce and defenseman Mike Robitaille. Imlach may have known what he was getting before anyone else had figured it out, as he suggested Don had the instincts of one of Punch's favorites on his Stanley Cup–winning Maple Leafs of 1967.

"When I met him again at training camp Punch said he remembered me playing in Kitchener because his son Brent had been playing junior at that time," Luce said. "He said he'd always appreciated the way I played back then and he was happy to get me. So that was the start of it. When I made the team, Punch asked me if I had a number in mind. I didn't, so he said, 'Would you mind wearing No. 20?' I said no, but is there a reason? He said I reminded him of Bob Pulford. So that's how I got my number.

"When I got there, Punch was still coaching the team and he had this persona of being this hard-bitten guy, but he was a good coach. I didn't actually play for him that long because he had the heart attack. As a coach, I enjoyed playing for him. And when he was general manager, back in those days, most of the players had agents. I didn't have an agent, so I had to deal with him. I had to negotiate my own contracts. I really got to know Punch. He would call me up in the summertime and he would ask me to come down, and we'd spend the whole day. We'd just talk hockey and stuff, and it seemed we talked more about hockey and less about my contract. It would go on for like three weeks, and so I got to know him pretty well. He was a very fair guy and a very straightforward guy, and he was a great person to play for and to negotiate contracts with. I did it myself and I didn't even have a lawyer look over my contracts."

Imlach always told players they would get the same amount in a contract whether they had an agent or not. "If you want to give some of your salary to an agent, then that's your business," he would say. "I never saw an agent score a goal, or stop a puck; but—hey—it's a free country." It's quite possible Luce got a better deal from the bald GM than some players with agents since Punch vehemently disliked dealing with them.

In his first Buffalo season Luce centered various line combinations, starting with Danny Lawson as one of his wingers. "That first year was kind of all over the map," he recalled. "Then Craig Ramsay got called up from the minors and there was more line juggling. But we killed penalties together, so Craig became the left winger on the line. The next year, we were paired with Larry Mickey, who was our right winger for a while. And then it became Rick Dudley, and then, of course, Danny Gare. Later on, after 'Tickets' [Gare] was traded, it was Rick Seiling. I had some very good line mates, which made it easier, and it was a very close-knit team.

"I don't think I've ever seen anybody that loyal to his team than Punch. If there was a trade, he would look to get you back. He got me back from Toronto, because he was extremely loyal that way, and he had a fierce desire to win, which filtered down to the players and to the organization. We all had it to a certain degree, but he had the fuel burning and he was a good part of that team. I think some of the players didn't realize how loyal and how much he did for them and how much he cared. There were times he helped players and I think he was misjudged a lot of times. He had the persona of being this hard-nosed kind of guy and he wanted that image.

"That's okay because when you got to know him, he was a lot more. He never put demands on a 10-goal scorer that weren't reasonable for a 10-goal scorer. All he would want you to do was to have your 10 goals. He didn't ask a 10-goal scorer to be a 20-goal scorer. He was very knowledgeable and reasonable in his demands. If you did that—if you delivered that—then he was just going to be loyal to you because that's all he'd ask of you and if you did it, you couldn't do any more."

The Penalty Killers

Don Luce and Craig Ramsay were about as good a regular pair of penalty killers as ever played the game, particularly when they also were the Sabres' second best offensive line and played a regular shift as well as killing off the short-handed situations. They made it an art as well as a science, often turning tables on the opposition, scoring instead of being scored on.

Luce recalled: "I did kill penalties in junior, but coming up to the pros, I had been the third highest scorer in the league [OHA Junior A]. So I thought of myself as an offensive player. But when I got to the Sabres I saw I wanted every opportunity to play. I knew I had a knack for killing penalties. I had a sense for it, and so that helped. When you kill penalties, it's more of an art than people think. To do it properly takes some skill. It's not something to be put up on a stat or anything, but I think you have to have an intuition for it.

"Partly when Rammer [Ramsay] and I played on the same line, we got to know each other's little nuances and where each other would be at certain times. Back in those days when the puck was shot in, I was the bigger player and I guess the stronger player, and so I wanted to go in and bring the puck away. Rammer was a little niftier and quicker in the forecheck, so he'd do that and I'd do the other part. It was just that we got to know each other pretty well and I knew where he was going to be if the puck was in a certain situation and in an area where he was going to get it. He knew if he forced a player in a certain way or he had the puck, he knew he would get it to an area where I was going to be. It made it very much easier for us to play it because you get a feeling for a person and you don't actually have to see them. I knew Rammer. He was going to be sneaking out here, and so I'm going to throw it out there, and he's there. So, it was easier because we did a real good job of killing penalties. It was a lot of fun to do. You've got to be on your toes all the time. It was an exciting part of the game for us. It was an important part of the game, too."

Ramsay reflected on being teamed with Luce and Gare: "One of the most underrated accomplishments in our league was the 50 goals [in 1975–76] by Danny Gare, playing on a line with us. That's because he sat the times that Donny and I killed penalties. The first year together they [Luce and Gare] both had 30-plus. The next year we had 100 together. You're never going to see that again. When you look at players now who are checkers, they get three or four goals. We had such a high-powered offensive team, everybody wanted to get involved. We were allowed to get involved offensively, not just be a checking line."

Luce was the king of the surprise goal: "The most short-handed goals I had in a season was eight [once an NHL record]," he said. "One game I'll never forget. We were playing Washington, and Rammer scored the first goal, short-handed, and then I scored the next two, both short-handed on the same penalty. And then I scored the fourth goal when we were even-up, so we won, 4–0. That was a lot of fun. It's exciting when you get chances to score. When you score on a penalty kill, that's a big momentum thing for your team. It can get you back in the game or it can get you out of a jam, or it can do a lot of things for your team."

Luce played most of his career in Buffalo, was traded to Los Angeles by Scotty Bowman in the late season of 1981, and true to Imlach's word, was brought to Toronto by Imlach the next fall, where Punch had returned for a second run as coach of the Leafs.

Luce shared his take on being a pro player: "It's almost like a kid living his dream. You grow up. I think when you grow up and have your job playing a sport, I don't think you can beat it. If you love something you do, and you're an adult and you are earning your living at it, it's just tough to beat. It's extremely satisfying. The people you meet playing…I can't compare it to anything else."

Luce was Perreault's teammate for a decade, as they were the two best centers on the team. He evaluated No. 11: "First and foremost, he's a great guy. You know, as an individual, a human being, he's one of the best. And that made it a lot easier, because he is extremely talented and one of the best players of that era. He was fun to watch as a player. Back then he could take the puck end to end better than any other player. He played a great game, but the best thing was he was a great guy, a great teammate. He was that way on and off the ice, a lot of fun to be with. You couldn't ask for a better superstar."

Gare Gets 50

When Luce and Ramsay played a regular shift, their line mate on right wing was Gare, who had one of the hardest wrist shots in the league. He had fast developed into a dangerous offensive player through hard work and a tenacious, disruptive style.

"Much of it was balance," Gare said. "I used to shoot a lot of pucks when I was younger and even when I was in the pros. I think kids don't do that as much anymore. When I watch them practice, they don't work on their shot when they're skating in. It's now more slap shots from a position. Saying that, my big strength was my wrists, you know, and my upper body. If I could get a goalie surprised by hitting an area or a hole, that's all I did. That's what I looked for, an opening. And quickness was a big part of it."

In his second year Gare was scoring in bunches, but so was Rich Martin, who probably received more media attention because of his place on the French Connection.

"My second year was huge, with Rico who had 49 [goals] going into the last game, and it was such a good story," Gare remembered. "I had 47 [goals] and we played at Philadelphia. We got beat 5–2, so I didn't really think about scoring 50, and Martin and [Freddie] Stanfield were saying to me, 'You never know.' Larry Carriere reminded me that when you get that close, you never know; don't think you can't. I really didn't think a lot about it. You know, maybe that was good. It just happened. Tiger Williams was lined up against me and said: 'You've got 47 and you don't have a chance.' I got really mad, and I just snapped. I was mad enough to at least try for 50.

"I scored one in the first and Rico didn't. In the second, neither one of us got a goal. In the third, [Sabres coach] Floyd Smith finally put me on the power play with Rico, who took a shot that I deflected up to the top shelf for a goal. I think everybody thought it was Rick's goal, but it was mine, so we both had 49. We went on a power play about three minutes later. We were lining up to get the rebound. It was one of those fabled goals. He was shooting. He wanted it, and I wanted it and I got it. I know I was pumped. I threw my gloves up and my stick and I never knew who I got the puck from. I think it was Lucey. Tiger's on the bench and I go by and say, 'Hey Tiger, that's 50, you dummy.' I lifted the puck up and he starts cursing me. So that was kind of a cool thing to get 50, but unfortunate for Rico."

The Goal Pad Incident

It was during their first playoff series that one of the strangest situations in Stanley Cup history came up. It was so bizarre that only a few of the 17,000 in the Montreal Forum knew what was going on. The Sabres were down three games to one when the teams faced off that night. The Canadiens were a magnificent team, with superstars such as Jacques Lemaire, Henri Richard, Jacques Laperriere, Guy Lafleur, and Ken Dryden. They had cruised through the regular season with only 10 losses during the 78-game schedule. But Imlach had a strange secret weapon that he was holding back for just the right moment.

Joe Crozier was in his first full year as the Buffalo coach. He had stepped behind the bench during the previous season when Imlach suffered a serious heart attack that nearly killed him, and ended his career as a coach in Buffalo. Punch was now the GM only, but he was very much a hands-on GM. The final visit of Montreal to Buffalo during the regular season seemed as routine as any other in the long NHL schedule. Except for one thing. I doubled as a Sabres practice goalie and was obsessive about the rules about goaltenders, had noticed something odd in Ken Dryden's equipment.

Dryden is a rangy, tall man, and his custom-made goal pads were longer than most goalies wore, to fit his legs properly. They were also wider, and there's the rub. At that time, the rule book said goalie pads could be a maximum width of 10 inches on the legs of the goalie. I was sure Dryden's were much wider than that, and I remembered that a goalie wearing illegal equipment could get his team a two-minute penalty. I rushed into Imlach's office to report my contention. Imlach was intrigued. "If this is true, we can save the knowledge for just the perfect moment; say in a playoff game when we really need a power play," he said.

"But we better make damn sure. You have to measure them and report back," he told me.

The Canadiens dressing room was locked for the few hours between the morning game day skate where the wide goal pads had been spotted, and late afternoon when the trainers would arrive to set up for the 8:00 PM faceoff. A member of the Buffalo training staff had a key to the Canadiens dressing room, for use when supplies or towels and so forth were delivered to the visitors. He opened the door and I went in with a companion. He strapped Dryden's goal pads on me and measured their width on my legs. They were slightly more than 12 inches wide. We carefully put the pads back, locked up, and ran back to Imlach's office to report. Punch smiled a Cheshire grin. "Next, make sure all our goalie equipment is legal. Since you started this, you tell our trainers it's their responsibility to make sure our equipment passes muster."

Goalie Roger Crozier's stick glove needed some minor adjustments, but all the other Buffalo goalie equipment, including— ironically—backup Dave Dryden's stuff, was okay. Yes, the name is familiar. Dave is Ken's brother, and he knew about the invasion of the Canadiens dressing room for pad measurement. "No way I would tell Ken," he said. "That's his problem. I play for Buffalo."

Late in the third period of Game 5 in the series, the score was tied at 2. During a stoppage in play, Sabres captain Tim Horton skated to referee Bruce Hood and spoke quietly in his ear. Hood immediately called Dryden to center ice and pulled out a measuring tape. "I knew the rule," Hood recalled a few years later. "I always carried the tape as I was supposed to do, but it hadn't been used for anything like a goal pad measurement."

Dryden's pads were too wide, by a wide margin, although Hood maintains they were more like 11 inches wide and not 12.

He called a two-minute penalty on the Canadiens, putting Buffalo on the power play. The Canadiens coach at the time was Scotty Bowman, who was infamous for finding ways to bend the NHL rules when it came to goalie substitution. He was furious behind the Montreal bench.

Regulation time ended with the score at 2–2. Up in the press box, no one but I knew what had happened with the goal pad incident. I was working as a commentator on the Sabres radio broadcast and confidently told listeners about the rule and the penalty. I couldn't tell them I had burglarized the Montreal dressing room to find out.

Scotty had been nearly apoplectic between periods. He went to NHL President Clarence Campbell's center ice seats and convinced Campbell to go to the Buffalo dressing room and demand a measurement of the Sabres goalie equipment. Campbell knocked at the door, but the feisty Imlach wouldn't let him in.

Overtime began with the Canadiens a man short. Lorentz had the first great chance to score. He recalled: "I could have been a hero. I came within about a half an inch of becoming one. During the power play I had an open net. With Dryden out of position, I shot the puck and it hit a defenseman's stick and hit the goal post. I still see that play."

A few minutes later, winger Rene Robert blasted a slap shot behind Dryden and the Sabres were back in the series. It was a shot and a game that made the NHL and the Sabres more than just an expansion team in western New York. The Sabres that night captured fans as never before. The series returned to Buffalo for Game 6. The author was honored by the players at their final banquet with his own gilded "goal pad measurer" made out of three pieces of wood.

"Nobody had given us much of a chance. But we certainly didn't feel that way. We took them to six games and that was one of the most exciting moments in my career," said Lorentz. "When the crowd stood in union and started chanting 'Thank You Sabres,' that was pretty special. It was spontaneous and totally unexpected, and for all of us to remember that, it shows you how important it was to the players."

Rene Robert recently told a Buffalo radio interviewer that the "Thank You Sabres" cheering in the Aud on that night was his "biggest thrill" in his hockey career. "Bigger than any overtime goal, or anything else," he said.

The Hawk Talks

There weren't many college players in the NHL during the early 1970s. The occasional player from a U.S. school made his way into the league, and those players were usually Canadians on athletic scholarship. Ken Dryden was one of them, graduating from Cornell University and then turning pro as a goalie.

It was rare that a player from a Canadian college was drafted, or even was invited to an NHL training camp. Canadian colleges and universities didn't have athletic scholarships in the early 1970s. Consequently, players in that hockey level were guys who most likely weren't pro prospects. One exception was Larry Carriere of Loyola in Montreal. In May of 1972 he finished a bachelor of commerce degree at the Jesuit school, and a month later he was picked 25th overall by Buffalo in the draft.

"I was a Montreal boy," he recalled. "On the day of the draft at the Queen Elizabeth Hotel, I went down there to hear Punch call my name in the second round. That same day, the Sabres picked Jim Schoenfeld in the first round. The team was building a great core of young guys who would take the team to the Finals in just five years."

Carriere started his first pro season in Cincinnati, but before Christmas he was recalled to Buffalo and stuck in the big leagues. "Punch liked young players, I think. He liked the way we were, full of energy and fun. I think he liked the fun part very much, although he was tough when he had to be," said Carriere.

Larry received his Buffalo nickname of the "Hawk" because of an obvious physical feature, a long thin nose that teammates jumped on immediately as a defining characteristic of the 20-year-old rookie. Good-natured and now in the NHL hockey business for 35 years, Carriere recalled his return to Buffalo after being traded to the Atlanta Flames.

"I had the good fortune to get married and buy my first home in Amherst when I was in my fourth year in Buffalo," he said. "Of course, as it always seems to go in hockey, as soon as I bought a house, I got traded. The day that happened, Imlach called me up to his office and told me to sit in his chair, behind his desk. I guess he wanted me to understand it's not always easy to trade a guy. 'I'm going to get you back here,' he told me. 'I just need to make this deal right now.' Darned if he didn't. Less than three years later he traded for me and got me back into a Sabres uniform."

Some trades cost a player money because he is anxious to sell a home when he moves on to another city. Carriere was sent to Atlanta shortly after his house purchase, but he was lucky enough to have Lee Fogolin as a Buffalo teammate. "When I was single I lived with Fogy, Danny Gare, and Morris Titanic," he recalled. "Then Sue and I got married, and I bought our first house. The day I was traded Lee said to me that he'd buy my house for the same price I paid for it. I agreed and went off to play for Atlanta.

"First time back in Buffalo I was anxious to play really well, to show Buffalo that they shouldn't have traded me in the first place. So I started hitting. First I hit Danny [Gare] and he hit me right back. Next, I hit Fogy pretty hard, and that turned into a fight. We had a pretty frisky go of it, and then were sent off to the penalty boxes where we sort of smirked at each other. Just that morning we had been together signing the final house papers and we were good friends. I could hear some of my new Atlanta teammates yelling from the player's bench: 'What's the matter, Hawk? Didn't you give him a good deal on the house?'"

Chapter 5
A Time for Sadness

"And Buffalo's a small town…so there is a familiarity that was there. And I love the fact that people made us part of that. We really felt we were part of that community."

–Jim Schoenfeld

Getty Images

Tim Horton (2) peers over the shoulder of teammate Jim Schoenfeld (6) as goalie Roger Crozier looks on in a game against the Maple Leafs in the early 1970s.

Horton and Schoenfeld

When the Sabres reported to training camp in St. Catharines in the fall of 1973, the team would seem to have been just right for a run further in the Stanley Cup playoffs. Gil Perreault was a genuine star in the league. Rico Martin had joined him in the constellation. Don Luce and Craig Ramsay were the preeminent penalty-killing duo of their time. Jim Schoenfeld—he of thunderous checks and a budding pop music career—would be in his second season.

"Schony" was Jim's nickname and he calls himself that to this day. He told of how one teammate was his friend and his teacher: "At my first training camp, the best thing that happened was that I ran into Tim Horton. Punch had drafted me, and Punch had brought Tim to the team and they were partners. He was a mentor to me and it was—It couldn't have been better. You know, if you want a teacher, he was extraordinary and at the first exhibition game, we were actually rooming together. And we had our pregame meal, and I came back to the room and there is Tim in bed already with the covers up around his chest, and he is reading a book and no TV on or no music, so I get down on my bed. I don't know what to do, and I must have lain there for about 10 minutes and I was convinced my breathing was too loud. So I said, 'I have to get up.' So I just got out of the room, and I don't know if that's what he would have wanted, but I didn't want to disturb Horty. He was reading his book and I was lying there trying to be as quiet as I could, but I thought he could hear me breathing so I thought I have to get up and out of this room. So I hung out for a while and waited for the bus to take us to the game.

"Horty was my mentor in my first season of '72–'73. I grew up watching him, so it was a very big deal to me that we were playing together. And the next highlight of that year would have been the last game against St. Louis. It put us in the playoffs and it was the team's third year. They didn't make it in years one and two, and I think it was a very big deal for everyone involved. And we went on to play Montreal and that series went six games, and they went on to win the Cup, I believe. We put a little dent in their armor and I guess we scared them a little bit, except the last game, we didn't scare them too much. Rico [Martin] scored a goal late in the game and that was it.

"I remember at the end of the game, the 'Thank You Sabres.' That was when fans were fans. Sometimes I think fans are just spectators, but the Buffalo fans were the best thing for our team and appreciated any effort put forth on their behalf. They knew we were overmatched. It was the Montreal Canadiens, for Pete's sake. We were a third-year expansion team. They were grateful for the effort of the players and coaches and trainer, the office staff. You know, it was a big deal. It became a very big deal in Buffalo, the hockey. I wasn't there the first two years but certainly from the time I was there, we became a real hot item. The fans really liked the team. There was an attachment to players. I've often said that the relationship changed very rapidly from player to fan to just friends.

"That's what I think of people from Buffalo, just the way they adopted you as one of their own. And Buffalo's a small town when you consider some of the big cities and you consider everyone you met went to school with or was a second cousin of someone you knew, so there was a familiarity that was there. And I love the fact that people made us part of that. We really felt we were part of that community. I also thought that [owners] Seymour and Norty [Knox] made it very special. I think they went out of their way to make it seem like a family.

"I remember when Seymour and Norty weren't doing so well, and there was a special night in their honor. So many of the guys came back, went on the ice to honor the Knoxes. I remember someone remarking when we were there during all the media interviews, and a reporter [said] it was just remarkable that all these players would come back. I said, 'That's just what family members do.' That's how we felt. When you talk about their legacy it has everything to do with that. They made us feel we were really part of something. It started with Seymour and Norty and it filtered through the team. Buffalo fans who became Buffalo friends. It was a great place for a young player, a great place to raise a family. As I say, you were just part of the whole. It was a good feeling in Buffalo."

The Album

Jim Schoenfeld was a heartthrob to hundreds—maybe thousands—of teenage Sabres fans. He received more mail in the front office than any player before, by a wide margin. Like most players then, Schony relied on front-office people to answer the bulk of the mail, and those writing in received a postcard-size black-and-white action photo of Jim as well as a Sabres window decal. It was the Sabres policy that every fan letter got some kind of reply, even the thousands that came from the Eastern Bloc countries in Europe. It used to cost about 50¢ in postage to send a 3¢ window decal overseas, but the Knox brothers insisted that Buffalo be known for its connection to all hockey fans.

Schoenfeld insisted the same about his connection. As a rookie, the big redhead had a girlfriend, who today has been his wife for decades. That didn't stop the mash notes from coming his way. To this day there are women in Western New York, now grandmothers, who still talk about their crush on Schony.

Jim personally answered as much of his fan mail as he could, but the task became overwhelming. He became more than a hockey figure in the Buffalo region. He was like a rock star by his second season.

Enter music. Schoenfeld recalled: "It's your normal interview in the dressing room when you're a first-year guy, and you're asked what you do in the off-season? 'Do you have any hobbies?' and that sort of stuff. Well, I play a little guitar. And Danny Neavereth got hold of the story and Danny, a popular local disc jockey in Buffalo, called me and said, 'Hey, you play guitar; would you like to make a record?'

"I wasn't smart enough to say no. I said, 'Why not?' I'll go down to a sound studio called Act One. I went in and played a little bit and sang a bit, and there was a terrific studio musician there, John Valby. He [John] did all the piano and all the synthesizer. I took my favorite group, the Beatles, and sang three or four of their songs. And that was payback for all the good listening they gave me. At the time it seemed like the thing to do. It was certainly a lot of fun. Unfortunately, it was recorded and it exists today. You know, some things you pay for over and over again. The only reason it was anything was because I was a Sabre. It certainly didn't stand on its own musical merits. That's for sure. It was a hot item, and as I said, it didn't matter what we did, people loved us. And as good or bad as it was, people seemed to like it. But listen, I had no false illusions about the music. I said if anyone wants it [the record], it's because I'm a player."

The Schoenfeld album, appropriately titled "Schony," still exists in private collections 35 years later. It includes a screaming version of "You Only Hurt the One You Love" with some of the most over-the-top reprise choruses in music history. But fans loved it. Disc jockeys in the Buffalo area played its songs throughout the rest of the second season, and Jim was asked to make club appearances—propositions he turned down. His teammates didn't rib him much about the album.

"They had as bad of musical taste [as I do], so it was okay," he said. "At least that's what they told me. There really wasn't that much teasing. It was just one of those things that was on and it's like news for the day, and then you go on to something else."

Horton Is Killed

After that first playoff run in the spring of 1973, the odds seemed to favor an even better season with a better team the next fall. However, the Sabres underachieved all winter long and came into Toronto for a game against the Maple Leafs on February 20, 1974, needing a win to stay alive in the hunt for a playoff spot.

Miles Gilbert Horton, alias Tim, was 44 years old that night and had told Imlach that this season was no doubt his last. His partnership with Ron Joyce in the donut store business was demanding even more time than before, as the chain was growing every month. Horton may have been a minority investor, but his name was literally on the buildings and he was determined to be successful as a businessman.

In the meantime, he was still a hockey player and, even at his age, one of the toughest, cagiest defensemen in the NHL. "He was my mentor. He was mentor to all of us," recalled Larry Carriere. "We had a young defense except for Timmy, and we learned things from him every day, about how to play the game and about how to handle ourselves as NHL players, on and off the ice."

Horton was almost always paired with second-year defenseman Jim Schoenfeld, the strapping 6'2" 215-pounder who arrived at the ice angry and then really got mad. Horton counseled Schoenfeld every day at practice to control his aggressiveness; not to get rid of it, but to make it work for him. Schony idolized Horton, and that's a fair word. Jim always wore his heart on his sleeve and had grown up in Ontario when Horton was a constant All-Star with the Leafs. His play and his class captivated Schony then and continued to do so when their lockers were close to each other in the Sabres dressing room.

"It was in the first period," remembered Carriere, "when Tim broke his jaw. He asked for a shot of painkiller and then came back out to play through the second." Horton-less in the third, the Sabres fell to the Leafs and were sent busing down the Queen Elizabeth Way, a beaten and discouraged hockey team. However, Horton wasn't with them on that team bus. He had stayed behind, in pain and maybe woozy from the painkillers, to meet with business partner Joyce in the Maple Leaf Gardens Hot Stover Club, a private membership lounge for those rich enough to afford it.

There's dispute about what happened next. The Ontario Provincial Police released a medical report a few years ago that asserted Horton had some very strong substances in his body that night, a large amount of vodka and drugs including antidepressants. The OPP reported he was being chased by police at speeds over 100 miles per hour on the QEW near St. Catharine's. The chase ended when Horton hit a concrete rail in his DeTomaso Pantera two-seater and flipped the vehicle, throwing him from the car. He was not wearing a seat belt and was dead at the scene.

Police called me, whose name they found in a media guide, and passed on the news. Imlach was called, as was Sabres coach Joe Crozier. "We didn't find out until we gathered for practice that morning," said Carriere. "It was devastating."

Craig Ramsay remembers hardly believing it. "He had been on the ice with us 12 hours before," Ramsay said. "And now he was gone."

Imlach was distraught. He had paid a signing bonus to Horton for his last contract. The bonus was the Italian sports car for a guy his friends knew liked to drive much too fast. Punch considered Horton a friend, not just a hockey player on his team. He was beside himself with grief.

The Horton funeral a few days later in Toronto attracted thousands, who gathered outside the crowded church to pay their respects to one of the greatest Maple Leafs of all. But Horton had died a Sabre, and his death also put the Buffalo hockey community into mourning. Though his number wasn't formally retired until decades later, Horton's No. 2 jersey was never issued by any Sabres trainer in the meantime.

Schoenfeld remembers his pain this way: "That was the season Gilbert broke his ankle and the year I had my back surgery. My wife, Theresa, and I were living in Fort Erie, renting one of the beach houses. I got the call early in the morning and I had just come back playing for a short time after I had my surgery. I got the call and it was like a fist in the gut. It wasn't like it was a situation where I did anything. I was almost frozen. And we had a game that night. So I just took the dog and walked up and down the beach in the middle of winter in the ice and the snow. I had to come to grips with it and I had to get the emotional part over with. And then I came back and grabbed the shovel. There was a big snow pile and I just moved it from one side to the other. I guess that's what you do when you're a player. You need something physical to do and slowly I thought "I'm okay," and I didn't have an emotional breakdown, and I was devastated but I was in control.

"I went to the Aud that night and I started the game. I was on the ice for the anthem and they asked for the minute of silence for Horty and that's when it hit me. It was unbelievable. It was almost as if I felt the combined grief of everyone in the building. I think everyone had a very high regard for Tim and it just overwhelmed me. Here I was standing there and tears were flowing down, and they dropped the puck, and I remember the puck came to me and I passed it off to somebody and finished the shift and came to the bench, and there's Joe the Crow. He came down and put his big old arm around me and that sort of was it, you know. It was just overwhelming; but hey, emotion hits you when it hits you, and you do your best to handle it. And then I was an honorary pallbearer. And there were a lot of us. It doesn't make me special, but it was very nice. I was really honored. People throw that word around, but it was truly a great honor for me to be included.

"It's funny to talk about a lifelong effect, but when I saw him in the coffin I made up my mind right then that I would never ever be put in a coffin. I could be burned or put me on a raft, put me out to sea and shoot an arrow with fire, because it just didn't fit him. He was too strong. He was big. He was too full of life and he looked so confined in there. But of course that's how we all did it in those days, and again I went home and that night I told Theresa, 'You know, when it's my time, you can put a torch to me.' It was funny, you know, funny how something like that could still last till this day."

Roger Neilson

One coach who wasn't a good ol' boy plied his trade in Buffalo and many other NHL jobs. The late Roger Neilson was the most innovative coach in the modern NHL and one of the great characters in the sport. The word *character* usually denotes someone who is eccentric and offbeat. Roger was all of that. But it was his character, his basic kindness and friendliness, that make him a foremost figure in all of what's good about professional hockey. As he battled cancer in the last years of his life, Neilson never turned inward or showed he felt sorry for himself in any way. He was a devout Christian, but he never wore his beliefs on his sleeve. He just acted them out, and his teams were the better for it. Any way you want to judge Roger on character, he comes out an A-plus.

He is credited by many with designing the so-called trap defense in hockey, a defense that, combined with illegal obstruction methods, slowed the game to a crawl in the late 1990s and the early part of this century. It's unfair to blame Roger, as he didn't promote the idea of making the trap better with holding, hooking, and interference. He basically spread five players across the neutral zone, facing the other team as it carried the puck up ice, and told his players to check the puck away. It is somewhat akin to watching paint dry, and its latter-day practitioners nearly killed the appeal of the world's fastest team sport by using it all the time.

Roger was once called "Captain Video" by the media. He came to the Sabres to coach under Bowman, who gave up the job to concentrate on being general manager. Neilson moved around to many jobs before and after Buffalo and once coached the Toronto Maple Leafs, the Sabres' fiercest rival. Roger believed shooting video of every game would help him break down the play as a coach and would be valuable for his players. In Buffalo, he hired a young Canadian hockey buff, Al Dunford, as a full-time cameraman and editor. Dunford was on the job at every game, home and away. Portable television cameras were heavy and cumbersome then. None had built-in videotape recorders as they do today, so Dunford was forced to lug a heavy external deck, plus a heavy camera and tripod, from one city to another. Even though games were on TV, Roger wanted wide shots of the play, even wider than the game camera in ordinary commercial coverage. He pored over the videotape and used it regularly in postpractice sessions with his team.

A lifelong bachelor, Neilson was too obsessed with his job to allot time and energy to marriage and children. But he always managed to have a pet dog. In keeping with a personality that reached out to everyone, Neilson adopted strays off the street. The most bedraggled was a tan mutt he named Mike, who came with him to Buffalo.

There was no specific rule against bringing pets into the Sabres offices. Norty Knox would sometimes show up with his sleek pair of black Labrador retrievers, and no one objected. Since he was an owner, who would object? But Mike was a different breed, or lack thereof. He hadn't been subjected to many baths during his undetermined years on this planet, and his fur was mottled and mangy. He once got caught in a fire, and though he wasn't seriously injured, Mike's hair was singed from top to bottom. Roger liked him despite his lack of sartorial splendor, and he brought the dog to the Sabres offices regularly. Sabres coaches always had two offices, one next to the team's dressing room and the other up in the Hockey Department at the front of the Aud, space shared with all of the franchise's other administrative functionaries, including the Knox brothers. One summer day a memo circulated to all employees from above, indicating proper attire (that meant shirts and ties) must be worn by all male employees in the office during business hours. It was aimed at Roger, I thought, who would come to work with no tie on and Mike in tow. The next day, Roger showed up in shirt and tie, and right behind him Mike strolled across the carpet, wearing a neatly tied cravat around his scruffy neck.

A career coach, Neilson began with great success in junior hockey at Peterborough. He was known for his ability to get a team to overachieve the first year he coached them. Sometimes the magic lasted two years. But sooner or later he would get the axe. They all expect the axe in the NHL, and Roger was no exception. He was unfazed by moving from city to city, usually leaving behind new friends who were more upset by his firing than he was. He looked like a serious Harpo Marx, with out-of-control curly hair and an avuncular style. Roger was one of the wittiest men I knew and could deadpan any kind of joke. When he died in 2003 one of the sport's most competitive and kindest—hardly a usual combination—left us behind.

Chapter 6
Wrestling With the Game

"If I can make a deal that improves a position on my team just 10 percent, then I am getting better. Ten percent here, 10 percent there, and soon I have a much better team."

–Punch Imlach

During his years as the Sabres' television analyst, Pat Hannigan recalled that hulking Australian wrestler Fred Atkins' workout and conditioning methods, which Atkins adapted for NHL players, were legendary.

The Terminator...Almost

He filled the room. His massive head blocked much of the sunlight from a picture window. His hands appeared to be the size of a pair of hockey gloves, but instead of colored leather, they were gnarled, scarred—fingers splayed by fracture, sprain, and pain after 50 years of serving as weapons in the wrestling ring.

Fred Atkins was truly a physical giant, not a grotesque, but an awesome chunk of humanity. He reminded me of the late Fred Gwynne, a television actor who played an amiable Frankenstein with platform shoes, a prosthesis head, and shoulder pads that made Gwynne lurch through scenes as a friendly grizzly bear.

Fred Atkins had it all for real. He stood about 6'6" or so and was Hummer-wide. His leonine head was topped by jet black hair, the result of dye job after dye job from his days attempting to remain youthful in the fast-turnover world of professional wrestling. Fred was an Australian who came to North America to pursue the bucks available to successful professional wrestlers in the days when Gorgeous George turned the sport from sport to exhibition.

Fred didn't wrestle as a clown or a good guy or even a bad guy. He wrestled in the days when there were real matches. Even if the winner might be predetermined, the wrestlers really did put on a show of wrestling. In short, they beat the hell out of each other and had a beer afterward. Atkins had been introduced to the yearling Sabres midway through their first season, after Punch Imlach had seen his roster crammed with drinkers, smokers, has-beens, and never-will-bes drop too many games just on conditioning alone.

As late as 1970, pro hockey was a self-contained sport. The money was lousy, and most players worked summer jobs back home pumping gas in an Ontario outpost or (if they were lucky) shilling beer at Canadian taverns that still had separate men's tap rooms and no doors on the bathroom entrance. The point was, one could surmise, that most who drank there didn't care about privacy in the loo. Those who played hockey for a living stayed in reasonable shape in the off-season, which extended from May 1 (if you were lucky enough to play on a team that survived to late playoff rounds) until Labor Day. But the word is *reasonable*. A summer with heavy lifting confined to beer glasses meant that first part of training camp was devoted to dry-land training.

Camps were usually held in backwaters all over Ontario and Quebec, one-burger towns with the main drag boasting a Canadian Tire Store and a pub inevitably named the "Kings," "Queens," or "Princess" hotel.

The fight for jobs and league level took place on the town's junior hockey arena ice, and thousands of Canadian boys caught their first glimpses of professional players in those freezing barns. Training camp opened with a week or two of just conditioning and intersquad scrimmages. Camp usually included running over hill and dale (despised by all) with the idea being to develop lung strength and get in shape for the season ahead.

The coach and the trainer usually supervised the workouts. Since major league teams trained with all their contract players and amateur tryouts under the same rink roof, minor league coaches and staff helped oversee the training regimen. Naturally some players devised clever and creative ways to avoid running and other muscle exertion that didn't happen on the ice with a puck and a stick. Players would disappear into the woods on a three-mile run, get picked up in a car by a friend, and show up minutes later sprinting across the finish line.

They did all these kinds of things in Buffalo's camp until Fred Atkins showed up on the heels of a home loss in which the Sabres were so hung over and lackadaisical that Imlach couldn't talk about his players without an every-other-word obscenity.

Atkins had already worked with many hockey players in his Crystal Beach, Ontario, home. Crystal Beach was home to an amusement park that served generations of tourists who crossed by excursion boat from Buffalo and rode the Comet Coaster or danced to the big bands in the park's Starlight Ballroom. But a day at Fred's house was more like a day on the rack for the unwilling. Fred's gym was in the basement of his modest bungalow near the Lake Erie shore, and some called it a torture chamber. Atkins offered a back-breaking workout for those with the right attitude, and it was understood you didn't go there with the wrong attitude. Two ex-players for the old American Hockey League Buffalo Bisons, Pat Hannigan and Bill Dea, who lived year-round near Fred, had worked out with him for years in the off-season and recommended Atkins. Hannigan, who later became a Sabres TV analyst and died in December of 2007, told the Toronto *Star* in 1983 that if he had discovered Fred earlier in his pro hockey career, the Atkins method might have made him a 10-year big-leaguer, instead of the four seasons he had with the Rangers and Flyers.

What was the Atkins method? Fred told the *Star* that same year: "A hockey player is the same as any other athlete. The trouble with them is, they've never been in shape. They've concentrated on building muscles, you see, when in athletics you have to be quick—and you lose quickness by lifting weights. I turn them around, get 'em stretching ligaments."

That was not all Fred stretched in his tiny basement gym. He once told a friend that blood had flowed off the basement's walls, "and it wasn't mine."

Now here's where you have to get something straight.

Fred didn't just talk a conditioning game. He didn't just look mean. He wasn't just an old beat-up shell of a pro wrestler, scamming money—or truly earning it—off athletes and coaches with his glare and quaint Aussie accent.

Fred Atkins in his seventies was the toughest son of a bitch in the world.

Or if he wasn't, consider this: One of the most famous wrestlers in the history of the sport—a champion before it became vaudeville—was Whipper Billy Watson. His take on Atkins when Fred was in his seventies and ready to work with the Toronto Maple Leafs at their training camp in 1983: "Even today I would say that Fred Atkins would defeat 90 percent of the wrestlers in the business. He was the toughest, best-conditioned wrestler I ever saw."

That was a decade after we met with Fred. He came to Buffalo. He saw...and wow, did he conquer.

When Imlach signed up Atkins, the Sabres practiced most off days at the Nichols School Rink on the city's north side, about a 15-minute ride from their Memorial Auditorium home. Nichols was (and is) Buffalo's high-end prep school, hardly expected to be the place where professional hockey players would find a welcome mat for their less-than-cultured approach to life.

To make that clear, the language used by most pro hockey players is not in any lexicon at Nichols. Most can't say a complete sentence without using at least one obscenity, blasphemy, or vulgarity. But Nichols it was, thanks to the school's prep hockey program that resulted in about the only available rink in the city besides Memorial Auditorium in the 1970s. Since Nichols wasn't designed as a home for a pro hockey team, the Sabres worked out in a gymnasium and then had to put on their hockey equipment (sans skates) and walk across the campus to the rink for practice.

First, though, they met Fred about 9:30 in the morning. Fred came to work with light equipment. His favorite workout apparatus was a stick about 24–30 inches long. Give a man a stick and Fred's instructions, and he would soon be in shape.

The Atkins method called for manipulation and contortions with that stick to stretch every muscle group in the body, making those groups more supple, more flexible, and stronger, with the result making a player less susceptible to injury.

His other tool was the players themselves. He would pair them off to do flexibility and strength exercises, pushing and pulling against each other, sometimes using the stick and sometimes not.

When Fred caught a player goofing off, he would call him by a formal patronymic.

"Mr. Martin," he would say. Stretching the "mister" like a rubber band, an Aussie accent larded with cynicism. "Missssssterrr. Mar-tinnnnn, would you kindly do something beyond sitting on your fat arse?" The Atkins glare would shrivel the culprit into submission and result in immediate action on the exercise.

One morning in the days when I served as a practice goalie for the Sabres, I was paired at the workout with a player named

Steve Atkinson. Stevie was what one could uncharitably call a "floater." He had good skills, good hockey sense, and some scoring ability. But he didn't have the work ethic needed to succeed beyond the level of a fringe NHL winger. That's why he had been available from St. Louis on waivers early in the Sabres first season. He hadn't improved much in his first two years with the team. Atkinson was not what one would call a hard worker in physical training or in practice.

That morning Steve figured that I was a perfect partner for the exercises. I was in my early thirties, no way a pro athlete, and sure didn't want to bust my hump in the workout. After all, I was the public relations guy, and we were supposed to be soft. He was right, but Fred didn't see it that way. He stood over us as Steve half-heartedly pushed the soles of his feet against mine while we both held on to the stick held straight out ahead of us.

If you push hard in this drill you stretch many muscle groups, and the work is hard and rewarding. If you don't push hard, and just sit there, it helps reduce the pain from too many beers and cigarettes the night before.

"Misss-terr At-kin-son," bellowed Fred. "Get to work, or do I have to do your bloody work for you?"

Steve glanced up at the standing giant and made a giant mistake. "Bleep you, Freddie," he said. Then Atkinson sneaked a smirk. The combination was perfect. It set Fred off like a fire horse when the alarm sounds.

Atkins showed the strength we all suspected was his. He leaned over to Atkinson, who was facing me foot to foot on the floor, and grabbed Steve by the scruff of the neck. Then he picked him up off the floor a few inches, as if Steve were a cat. But he was a 185-pound man, and he was helpless in the hold of the old wrestling giant.

I don't know whether Fred Atkins was using some kind of paralyzing wrestling hold, but when he dropped Atkinson back onto the carpet, Steve was limp for several seconds, and there wasn't a sound in the gym.

The other players were dumbfounded, and so was I. I have

never seen an act of greater strength by a man.

For the next year of Fred's position as strength trainer, the Sabres not only got better, stronger, and more flexible and suffered fewer injuries, but they also remained in grudging awe of a man old enough to be their grandfather.

Only a few remember Fred as a hockey trainer, but he is in the Canadian Wrestling Hall of Fame.

Eddie Iceberg and the Turtle

Eddie Iceberg and the Turtle were with us for one season. You won't find their names in the record book. They couldn't skate and they weren't even players. But for one unique season, they were on the team.

Punch Imlach had a reputation as one of hockey's traditional hard-bitten taskmasters, an old-school guy who did it by the book—his book, anyway. But he often surprised us with innovation. In the late 1970s after the Sabres had advanced to the Stanley Cup Finals for the first time and had been defeated in six games by the Philadelphia Flyers, Imlach decided he needed to do something, anything, to raise the level of his team's play a notch higher. He had a solid mix of talent, and he kept nipping and tucking at the roster to produce a champion. The problem seemed to be that every improvement in the team was reflected in a loss of talent in another area, so Buffalo still couldn't get over the hump. Goalie Roger Crozier, the backbone of the defense, retired due to illness, while Tim Horton was killed in an automobile accident after a game in Toronto.

Traditionally—and Imlach knew it—teams win on the total accumulation of talent, not so much the intangibles fans think are important. Imlach dealt with building an expansion on the roster, not on coaching, team spirit, and morale; a roster loaded with everyone else's rejects. That team was a Stanley Cup finalist after five seasons, and he did it one little bit at a time.

"If I can make a deal that improves a position on my team just 10 percent," he said, "then I am getting better. Ten percent here, 10 percent there, and soon I have a much better team." Take note of the "I" in the Imlach statement. Punch was never shy about taking credit for the teams he headed. "If they don't like the way I do my job," he told me, "then fire me. But leave me alone in the meantime." The Imlach will and the Imlach ego were nearly legendary in the world of professional hockey. There was grudging admiration for both his skills and his luck. Recall his mantra that "I'd rather be lucky than good." That's what he told the media after winning the lottery wheel spin that gave him the right to draft Gilbert Perreault in June 1970, a pick that gave Buffalo the best forward in franchise history, a future member of the Hockey Hall of Fame.

But Punch didn't always count on his luck. Just when you thought you had him figured out, he would do something different, unusual, or even outrageous. That's what happened with the Turtle and Eddie the Iceberg.

They were more formally known as Allan Turowetz and Ed Eisenberg, a pair of Canadian academics with a variety of psychology degrees and jargon to match. They were both hockey fans and had conceived of a consulting business in which they would teach team building in the NHL and all of pro sports. In short, they were sports shrinks for hire. Bring Allan and Eddie aboard your franchise ark, and they'd work long and hard to build camaraderie while collecting fancy professional fees to do the job. When you go to a lawyer and ask him if you need his services, do you think he'll ever say no? Once you ask, you're hooked for at least one big fee. Of course you need a lawyer, you'll be told, that's why you're here!

It was the same with Eddie and Al and those who have followed in their team consultant path for the past three decades. 'Of course you need us,' they point out. If you didn't need us, you wouldn't have thought to talk to us, let alone hire us. Imlach didn't seem to be the kind of guy who would readily latch onto this kind of logic, let alone hire psychologists to massage the players' egos on the Sabres. Yet here he was.

It seemed that Imlach knew he only had a few more kicks at the cat as a hockey executive. He had nearly died from a heart attack in the 1971–72 season, and the cast of characters and character players he had assembled in Sabres blue, white, and gold five years later was one of the best rosters in the NHL. But they were frayed at the seams, without the core of a championship team, a proven Cup-winning goaltender.

More than that, Imlach was very superstitious, sentimental, and a gambler at heart and at wallet. He put his money down on ponies, geldings, mares, and stallions at race courses across the continent, including one day at Bowie, Maryland, where sentiment and good sense collided, with sentiment winning. The horse was "Tim's Song." The trainer was from Saint Catharines, Ontario, the city where the Sabres usually trained and the scene of the auto crash that had killed Tim Horton in 1974. Horton was not only one of Imlach's favorite players in Toronto and Buffalo but also an old friend. His death had affected the usually crusty general manager deeply. To top it off, the race colors of "Tim's Song" were blue and gold.

"Do me a favor," he said to me. "Take this and put it down on that horse to win." That horse was going off at 50-to-1 or so, the longest of long shots, but Imlach said he couldn't pass up the chance to bet a nag so obviously named after his friend and former defenseman, the late Tim Horton. I placed the bet and returned to watch the race with Punch and then Sabres coach Floyd Smith. I hoped the horse could sing, because he needed another career after finishing that race dead last, 15 or so lengths behind the winner.

Punch wasn't disappointed at losing, as he had honored a memory with his hunch bet.

That gambling instinct convinced him to spend about $50,000 of the Knoxes' money on a scheme that was so preposterous it could work. The Turtle and Eddie Iceberg were outwardly a decidedly unmatched pair. Turowetz spoke at Gatling gun pace, firing words, phrases, and entire paragraphs at the listener so rapidly it was nearly impossible to pick up the gist of his statements. Eddie Iceberg was calm and measured in comparison, and superficially he was the sober-sided one in this odd couple. The Turtle's hair matched his personality, frizzy and flying off at so many angles that he appeared to carry a brown halo around his head. The Turtle was a real hockey fan, an insightful one at that. He thought he knew more about the game in the NHL than almost anyone outside the playing and coaching ranks, and he wasn't afraid to tell listeners what he knew. This Montreal native went on to coauthor a book on the Canadiens franchise just a few years later, so he had a buttoned-up mind on the sport. Some of us thought he had a few loose buttons at first, when he and Eddie Iceberg distributed long questionnaires to every employee, seeking answers to some personal queries as well as some that seemed just plain dumb.

The word came down from the Knoxes: "Fill out the question-naires, and don't fool around." I guess they were determined to get their 50 grand's worth. After the forms were collected, the "team shrinks," a title that they soon heard about and objected to mildly, scheduled individual meetings with every employee. At those meetings, the office staff was grilled about its relationship to the franchise, to the players, and to the fans. One couldn't help but be amused by the whole thing. On the face of it, the idea that this could get the team on the right track was a little preposterous.

But as the meetings ground on (there were many more with the players than with the front-office types), the team also began to win with regularity. Since I was part of both worlds (front office and dressing room), I heard every snide remark and joke about the hyperkinetic Turowetz and his more measured business partner, the cool Eisenberg.

Rene Robert, a gifted goal scorer and even more gifted club-house lawyer, was the most aggressive when it came to criticizing the Turtle and Eddie Iceberg. Robert didn't just stop there. He berated the Knox brothers and Imlach for "such a stupid [bleep-ing] idea in the first place." However, the Sabres kept on winning and, more importantly, winning on the road, where they had been less than adequate the season before. To have a real shot at a divi-sion title and a long run in the Stanley Cup playoffs, a team would have to play well on the road, with the hockey rule of thumb sug-gesting said team win 50 percent of the road points.

The shrink-laden Sabres were doing better than that. The Turtle and his partner were traveling with the team, and they would dance and hug each other with glee after every road win. You could almost see the dollar signs light up their eyes. What a world! Convince a franchise that simple psychological research methods could win hockey games. They immediately opened negotiations with other NHL teams (all pro sports are copycat operations), and the Turtle built air castles of million-dollar consulting contracts with the NFL, the NBA, and Major League Baseball. We heard all about them, delivered by Turowetz in those bullet-fast, bitten-off sentences. If one listened long enough, it was not hard to believe that the day of the team shrink was at hand, and the Turtle was its messiah.

Even the most skeptical of the front-office staff had only to check the NHL standings to see Buffalo at the top of the heap as the season wore on. It may have been sheer coincidence, but the Knox brothers were soon brushing aside remarks aimed at the shrinks, admonishing the cynics and nonbelievers to just look at the on-ice results.

Imlach was never a true believer, though he opined he would do anything to help his team win, and they were winning since the two academics had come aboard.

Punch was very superstitious and would never change anything in the middle of a winning streak. He wore those expensive Canadian beaver fedoras, and the same one was on his bald head every day until a streak was over. When one ended, he would walk into his office and casually toss the hat-that-lost-its-winning-habit across the desk to sit on a corner waiting for another rotation weeks or months ahead. "I don't know if the son of a bitch was giving us any luck," he once said to me, after putting a pale tan beaver hat in limbo following a loss, "but I sure as hell wasn't taking any chances."

Neither of the shrinks wore hats, at least not when they were around the Sabres. But they soon caught some of the illogical logic that makes pro sports go round. They would always sit in the same plane and bus seats on a road trip, and the Turtle would inevitably show up in the press rooms across the NHL for the pregame meal.

It could have been that he liked free meals. He liked mixing with media types so he could regale them with stories of the success of the Sabres under his and Eddie's regimen. Curiously, he never did much regaling on the road. The Turtle grew up in hockey-mad Montreal. NHL arenas (particularly the old Forum) were hallowed ground to the young Turtle, and he became inordinately quiet in each arena's inner sanctum.

But he was garrulous everywhere else, leaving his partner the second man in an ersatz Abbott and Costello routine. If you listened long enough, the Turtle would have tossed a bit of Hegel in with Bobby Hull and Gordie Howe, and Spinoza with Esposito. He burst into any setting like a New England blizzard, or more accurately, a lake-effect snow job hitting Buffalo. Eddie Iceberg would merely nod when his partner went off, an everyday occurrence.

Once we got to know them a bit, we used to tease them constantly about what they were getting paid for. More to the point, we used to badger them all the time about exactly what the hell they did.

Despite hours with the Turtle, we weren't able to separate the banter from the real thing, if there ever was a real thing. It all seemed like smoke and mirrors, what with all the questionnaires and interviews and group therapy sessions. Well, not quite the latter, but we were getting close.

One day I decided to see how much bull could fly around the shrinks before anyone in the front office would question what they were up to in trying to (in their words) "build organizational and team unity." I wrote a memo to all those in the front office, from the Knoxes to Evelyn Battleson, who was our switchboard operator. It said, in part: "Professors Turowetz and Eisenberg have asked that every employee do an inventory of all the objects on and inside their desks. It is felt that an analysis of these objects will better enable them to understand the emotional makeup and attitudes of all employees towards the organization and the team." I had the memo distributed (e-mail was just a twinkle in Bill Gates's eye then), and within minutes I was assailed by several secretaries who were very irritated.

"I don't mind doing my desk," one young woman told me, "but my boss wants me to do his, too. And that's a real pain. His desk is full of all kinds of junk. Some of it may even be dead."

We'll leave the identity of that boss a mystery, but I did find out that inventories were under way throughout the offices. Except for assistant general manager Fred Hunt, an old-school hockey guy who accepted the memo as real but refused to check out his desk, as he thought it was "just more of this damned psychology foolishness." When I told the Turtle of my inventory memo hoax, he bristled at first but then said it might not be a bad idea to add to their data bank of information on the Sabres. "Hey," I said. "My idea, so I get paid for it."

The tale of the Turtle and Eddie Iceberg ended that spring when the Sabres were unceremoniously bounced from the play-offs by the New York Islanders. Imlach didn't bring them back, but it hadn't been expected from the beginning. They did go on to do that voodoo they did so well with at least one team in the Canadian Football League, then went their separate ways. The Sabres weren't the only franchise to go through the day of the Turtle. And the book Turowetz later coauthored on his beloved Canadiens was a decent read, but the prose never captured his explosive, eccentric personality.

One Montreal radio station did find him intriguing, putting Allan on the air in a sports talk, phone-in format once a week. The professor was never stumped by his callers (think of Frasier Crane), although radio didn't become his career. It's difficult to imagine every listener being required to inventory his or her desk. But if the Turtle had thought of the idea before me, I don't doubt he would have tried it out on the radio audience.

Chapter 7
The Man Who Never Was

"Wouldn't it be great if someone would take a player who isn't even eligible for draft? They'd be screwed up in Montreal [league headquarters then] if they had to chase that one down."

–John Andersen

Taro

The NHL was at war with the young World Hockey Association, and the league's general managers agreed to a ploy that would serve as a tactical victory, if not a strategic one.

It was 1975, and in Buffalo general manager Punch Imlach couldn't have been more vocal about the NHL's decision to hold its entire entry draft over the phone. "Expletive, expletive, expletive NHL; expletive, expletive, expletive," roared Imlach whenever anyone even mentioned the draft.

The idea, presumably, was to keep each team's choices, as well as the round in which they took any player, secret. This was supposed to allow the NHL to sign players before the WHA even knew who was drafted in what round and thus, not be able to offer the kind of money needed to outbid a draftee from any particular round. If this sounds convoluted, so be it. The machinations of pro leagues at war with each other would cause a constitutional crisis if they were part of governing a nation. It came down to the fact that some teams are always cheaper than others—thus, some wouldn't go to the wall to sign a draftee in then NHL-WHA war.

On that early June day, general managers, coaches, and scouts waited patiently in every NHL office for the phone to ring so they could pick it up to hear NHL President Clarence Campbell sonorously announce on speakerphone: "(Team Name), it is your selection in the first round." No other team could hear the call to any succeeding team. Before each team drafted, Campbell would read off the names and teams of every player drafted since your team's last call. This made for an interminable draft. It took hours to get through the first two rounds, and exhaustion set in by late in the afternoon. In those days the NHL was operating a draft that went on as long as teams wanted to draft, which meant that the drafting would go into a second day.

If Imlach was angry about the first day, you could say *catatonic* was the description when Punch had to sit down and wait for a phone call on Day Two. The Sabres continued their call as the rounds went on, and though the drafting rounds moved more

TARO SAYS...
目標はスタンリイ杯

Taro Tsujimoto Bumper Sticker—Translation was "We're Gonna Win That Cup!!"
—Taro was a fictional player from Japan "drafted" by the Sabres in the 1974
Amateur Draft—The scam was the idea of Paul Wieland, Public Relations Director
of the Sabres. It drew the ire of League Commissioner Clarence Campbell

quickly each succeeding time, he was still furious. John Andersen was the Sabres' scouting director and sat alongside Punch. I was on the other side of him at a table and was in charge of informing the media of whom Buffalo had drafted as the rounds went on.

Andersen was Danish by birth and still had the curl of an accent from his native tongue. He also had a dry and laconic sense of humor. "Wouldn't it be great," he posed, "if someone would take a player who isn't even eligible for draft? They'd be screwed up in Montreal [league headquarters then] if they had to chase that one down."

"Wouldn't it be greater," I replied, "if someone drafted a player that didn't even exist? Can you imagine how that would screw up the crew in Montreal trying to find his draft eligibility?"

The player to be chosen?

That was the easy part. We could choose anyone we wanted to choose since we were creating the player from the wellsprings of our imaginations. How about someone from a country where hockey is played but certainly never would be producing NHL players?

How about someone from the Orient, say from Japan? They have hockey up in the north there, we knew, but on the world stage, the Japanese were merely stagehands. Japan had entered international competition and had routinely been destroyed by nearly every country its national team faced. So who would our player be?

"Taro should be his first name," Andersen said. "That's a relatively common Japanese name." I recalled there was an oriental market and gift store called Tsujimoto's in a Buffalo suburb. I checked a phone book for spelling, and presto, we had our player—Taro Tsujimoto.

Actual players have teams and stats, so Taro needed some. A phone call later to check on the rough translation of *Sabres* into Japanese and we had our team—the Tokyo Katanas—a nickname that we were told meant "Sabres" in Japanese.

As any good public relations man can tell you, stats are important. I made Taro 5'10" tall, with a weight of 175 pounds. He had scored 15 goals and 10 assists for the Katanas last year, numbers that are hardly imposing. They played a short season in Japan. We finished our creation of a hockey Frankenstein with the melodic name of Taro and sat back to wait for Buffalo's next drafting turn. Imlach tapped his fingers nervously on the long oak desk until we heard Campbell's droning voice.

"Next selection is Buffalo's. Is Buffalo on line?"

"Yes," Imlach replied, and we listened as Campbell recited the names of all the players and their amateur teams taken since Buffalo had chosen the round before. "Your selection, Buffalo?"

Imlach positively smirked, leaned toward the conference phone, and said: "Buffalo selects Taro Tsujimoto from the Tokyo Katanas."

There was a moment's silence. "Could you repeat that?" asked Campbell. Punch repeated the name. "Spell it, would you please?" Letter by letter, Imlach spelled it out, and Campbell repeated each letter. He was clearly perplexed, but there was no way he could challenge Buffalo's pick. Imlach, to Campbell's knowledge, hadn't drafted someone ineligible. He had no clue, so he had to go along.

The call ended, and we decided to keep the whole thing our little secret. I prepared a brief release on the selection that was distributed by phone to the local media who were interested. It made a good note. The Sabres had drafted a Japanese player, and he's believed to be the first from that country ever taken by the NHL. In the meantime, poor Campbell had to spell Taro's name and ID to every other team in the draft. There were 15 others, and we sat in the Sabres boardroom snickering every time we thought of the way the league president made his announcements.

"Taro...That's T-A-R-O...Tsujimoto...That's T-S-U-J-I-M-O-T-O...from the Tokyo K-A-T-A-N-A-S."

There were times in a quarter century in the hockey business that were frustrating. But there were other times when the sheer joy of goofing around with what is, after all, just a child's game played by men wearing short pants and ice skates could not have been matched by any Fortune 500 company job.

And this time with Taro was one of them.

Taro Comes to Training Camp?

The Taro draft was in June. That summer his name entered the NHL guide, where it stayed for the next 30 years as a Buffalo draft selection in the round after Derek Smith and before Bobby Geoffrion. Smith played in the NHL for several years, first with Buffalo and then with Detroit. When he found out that Taro was a hoax, he told us: "Thank God I went in the round before. What if it was in the round after?" Bobby Geoffrion, a son of Hall of Fame winger "Boom-Boom" Geoffrion, was selected in the next round and got a brief look at training camp that fall before being released. Geoffrion never knew that his draft was lower than the player who never was.

Smith recalled his draft experience: "I feel fortunate that I was able to beat Taro by one round, and he didn't even exist. I went late in the draft, 10th round. Right around that time Philly began to win the Cup. It was a different brand of hockey, so small guys who had been drafted a couple years before were usually a first or second pick whereas after Philly won the Cup, it kind of changed how teams drafted players. So that changed the way I was drafted. It worked out; it always works out. As it turns out, my father played two years with Punch Imlach with the Quebec Aces. One year Punch was the player/coach and the next year he was a player. And even when Punch drafted me, he didn't know I was Julian Smith's son. However, my dad did talk to him over the summertime to make sure he put a face with the name. That helped also."

Training camp that fall was Taro's finest hour. The team published a media guide for camp, to be held 40 minutes north of Buffalo in St. Catharines, Ontario. Taro was listed in the roster and given a uniform number.

He got more than that, thanks to Rip Simonick, the Sabres equipment manager (then and now) who was an old friend with a wicked sense of humor. Rip issued a full set of equipment to Taro, from long underwear and socks to two uniform jerseys. He was assigned his own stall in the dressing room. When other players reported to the first day's practice, Simonick told them Taro was expected in from Japan "any time now."

Seymour and Norty Knox hadn't been told about our draft-day joke that invented Taro. There was no conspiracy at first. It was as simple as the fact that neither was on hand for the second day of the draft. The entire coaching and training staff soon were conspirators, however, figuring that it would be funny if they deceived the bosses in a harmless prank.

Summer was vacation time in the NHL, with all trying to stuff what holidays they could between the amateur draft and training camp opening around Labor Day. The Knoxes still didn't know the truth about Taro. When the training-camp guide came off the presses, Seymour asked about the "Japanese player," would he be coming to camp?

"I think so," I told him, "but you might ask Punch or John." I left it in their hands to explain the Taro story. They did all right, telling Seymour that they weren't sure about Taro either, that we'd just have to wait and see. It was common practice for Seymour and/or Norty to spend time at training camp in the first few days of sessions. They would sit with Punch or team scouts, who would background them on the newest products of the Sabres farm system and draft. The rinks were always cold, and the brothers weren't any different from anyone else; they tried to warm up at midday by going out to lunch.

In 1975, training-camp headquarters was at the Holiday Inn

in St. Catharines. The second day of camp saw Seymour Knox join friends at a window table for a midday sandwich. Sabres Coach Floyd Smith was hanging out in the lobby with me when a young, athletic man of obvious Japanese extraction walked by and headed into the restaurant. "Are you thinking what I'm thinking?" Floyd asked. "It could be Taro," I replied. "By God, it must be Taro."

We walked over to the front desk and asked if it was possible to have an announcement put on the hotel public-address system, and would it be heard in the restaurant? The answer to both was yes. So we made our plan. When we could see the Japanese fellow was getting up to leave, we walked back to the front desk, and asked for this announcement on the PA: "Will Mr. Taro Tsujimoto please report to the front desk?"

Within a minute after the announcement, the Japanese man walked out of the restaurant and through the lobby, with Seymour Knox about five steps behind him and gaining fast. Seymour was chasing down Taro. Or so he thought, until he came upon Smith, who was convulsed in laughter. "Seymour...wait...wait," Smith said. "We have something to tell you."

Seymour joined the laughter after we explained that Taro was only a construct by three of his employees on a slow draft day. He and his brother Norty had not known what they were getting into when they hired Imlach and me in 1970. They thought they were getting one of hockey's best coaches and general managers (they were correct) and an experienced public relations practitioner (they were correct once more). But they didn't realize that putting Punch and me in the same space would result in some of the wackiest publicity stunts in pro sports history. Taro was just one of them—one that worked very well.

Filling the Seats

Imlach wasn't a prankster by nature, but he understood that his team and the young Buffalo franchise needed all the publicity they could get. First call, of course, was building a lineup that could challenge for the Stanley Cup. That was the only longtime strategic goal of everyone in the Sabres organization. In the meantime, we had to put fannies in the seats and try to establish an emotional attachment to the team and the franchise with a relatively small fan base. The Knox brothers had obtained the Buffalo franchise after bailing out the NHL by financially supporting the Oakland Seals, who were in danger of folding during the 1969–70 season.

Buffalo was a minor league market. That was the common opinion when the movers and shakers of the NHL met, and they had passed along that perception to the media, particularly the influential print and broadcast journalists in Canada. When the franchise was awarded to the Knox brothers, it was expected that the Sabres could only succeed if the team drew a major part of its fans from nearby southern Ontario. Otherwise, it would fall flat. Or so the critics wrote. But the Sabres organization didn't hold to that perception very long. In the first season of 1970–71, the team played in a Memorial Auditorium that held only 10,466 fans when stuffed to the rafters. An expansion of the building to major league capacity had been planned before opening night, but the funding couldn't be put together in time.

The Sabres' administrative vice president, Dave Forman, had been hired by the Knox brothers because he was both a smooth glad-hander and a dynamic get-it-done project manager. Forman even sold season tickets to the man on the street. If he saw someone at a Sabres ticket window, he would walk over and ask if he could talk about seeing all the games. Then he'd sit the fan down in the office, and by the time he was done, another season-ticket holder exited smiling.

That first year's team had a roster full of culls from the league's 12 clubs who were in existence the year before. Buffalo and Vancouver were both new franchises and were forced to take 18 of other teams' rejects and pay for the privilege. That's how expansion works in pro sports. One pays millions to get players who are fringe talents, and one must be prepared to suffer for a few seasons at least.

The first year in Buffalo was full of suffering for long periods.

Despite the talents of the first overall draft pick, rookie Gilbert Perreault, Buffalo languished in the East Division basement during the first half of the season, and fall attendance figures weren't encouraging. Buffalo fans had just come off winning the Calder Cup with the AHL Buffalo Bisons the year before, and they weren't used to seeing losing hockey, big league or not. Imlach was patient and clever. He began making trades that improved the team incrementally. Imlach rode the team he was assembling mercilessly. He had several players who were considered "bad livers" by other coaches, and at least two were borderline alcoholics who would show up for practice still full of booze from overnight partying.

Late in the season, Buffalo was blown off the Auditorium ice by a Chicago team that toyed with the Sabres and won by five goals. The Sabres were losing too often for Imlach, even though he knew he didn't have a team that could win regularly. He knew some of his veterans were just collecting paychecks, figuring this was the last season, as they'd already been discarded into Buffalo's roster and the team was certainly going to be made over at season's end.

Punch was always loyal to veteran NHL players because he knew how difficult it was to make the league when there were six teams, and it was still tough with 12 and 14 teams. He honored them more than they realized by giving them the leeway to have fun (translation: drink and carouse) as long as they showed up ready and able to play. That first Sabres team had several who were legends among their peers for partying habits. Allan Hamilton, a defenseman taken in expansion from the New York Rangers, had wasted great physical talent but could hug beer bottles as well as anyone in the league.

Tracy Pratt was another hockey playboy, and he had even been kept out of the United States at one point on a moral turpitude issue. Eddie Shack, one of the old Toronto Maple Leafs that Imlach traded for during the first season, was called "Eddie the Entertainer" for his on-ice antics. Shack was even better at partying than playing, and his gravely voice was known in a series of downtown Buffalo taverns, pleading with bartenders to forget about last call and just keep on serving.

The Sunday night of the Chicago debacle, Imlach returned to his downtown hotel suite angry and frustrated with his team. Whenever an Imlach team lost, Punch would be up late that night, reliving the game and often pacing the floor, sipping at some good Scotch himself. He would fume while he tried to figure out what changes he could make to improve the situation. His suite was on the side of the hotel that faced a Buffalo street that was the home of several joints open to the wee small hours. One pub was called Ace's Steak Pit, and it was just 75 feet or so away from the Imlach digs.

The noise level was always high inside Ace's, but not so much on the sidewalk in front. That early Monday morning, however, one voice cut through the cacophony as a bunch of drunks poured out the front door at closing time. It was Eddie Shack, leading most of his teammates, who were as drunk as he was, or at least they all appeared to be. Imlach wasn't surprised that the noise came from his so-called major leaguers. He decided what he would do in the morning, and then turned in for some fitful sleep.

The Worst Practice Ever

At 9:00 AM I strolled into the Sabres offices on the arena level at Memorial Auditorium and checked in with Punch, who was sitting behind his office desk absentmindedly slapping his palm with a letter opener. Mondays were usually my sure day to prac-tice in goal with the team, as Imlach gave the regular goalie, Roger Crozier, a pass from ice duty nearly every day after he played in a game. Roger was suffering from pancreatitis, a chronic disease that fatigued him. At about 5'7" and 140 pounds, the diminutive goalkeeper was the best player next to Gil Perreault on the roster and kept the Sabres in nearly every game he played. He was what's called a "gamer," a player who is at his best under the most trying of conditions.

He was named the Most Valuable Player in the Stanley Cup playoffs five seasons earlier while playing for Detroit, despite the fact that the Red Wings had lost in a six-game Final. Roger was as acrobatic a goalie as ever had played in the NHL, and he was a crowd pleaser, hanging off the crossbar at times to make saves. I was 180 degrees opposite, and then some. An amateur goalie of limited talents, I was still playing senior hockey in the Buffalo area when one day Imlach challenged me to suit up for a practice and fill in for Crozier. "You're kidding," I said to him, expecting it was some kind of joke. "Hell, no," he said. "Somebody's got to be in there and it might as well be you. Besides, you should be a morale builder."

What he meant was that it was very likely pucks would go by me in droves, helping his team to feel good about themselves. He was correct. My first times on the ice were my worst. Some of the kinder players got me aside after my first few weeks and told me to relax. A slightly built center, Billy Inglis, was the kindest of them all. "I think you're nuts," he said. "But if you're going out there, just take it easy and have fun. You don't have to prove you can play in the NHL because you can't. The guys think you have a lot of guts just to get out there with them. They respect you because you're going through what they go through." That leads me to the fateful Monday, after the Sunday night disgraceful loss to Chicago and Imlach's observations of his drunks leaving Ace's.

"You don't want to practice today, Paul," he said.

"Why not?" I replied. Punch's answer: "Because there isn't going to be a puck on the ice. I'll teach those bastards to play so lousy and then get drunk afterward. They're stealing the money. Well, today they're going to earn it."

I walked out of his office and thought for a moment. I knew the way I could gain more respect as a sort of fellow of the players and not just the public relations man was to stick to my practice schedule. If I didn't show up today, they'd realize I bailed out or was warned about how bad it was going to be. I was confident I could take anything Punch would throw at us. Boy, was I stupid not to skip the workout, and very sore because of it.

Practice that day was on the rink at the Nichols School on the city's north side. Personal connections with Sabres management allowed the rink to become available when needed. There was a problem, however, as the team had to dress in another building about 50 yards away, and haul sticks, gloves, and skates to the rink, then finish dressing at ice side. Goalies had it worst. We had to drag our big leg pads plus all the other goalie impedimenta from gym to rink and back again.

That morning we gathered in the cold, moist air of the rink. I could see hangovers were the order of the day. Slowly the bedraggled group got skates on and gingerly stepped onto the ice, skating tentative ovals at tentative speed. The Sabres backup goalie was Dave Dryden, who had come back into pro hockey after working as a schoolteacher near Toronto, spurred to return by more job chances due to expansion.

Dave was a well-conditioned athlete who didn't smoke or drink (a rarity among professional hockey players) and was alert and ready to practice, more than could be said for the rest of the team. I skated alongside him. "Dave, the bald guy [Imlach] says no pucks today. Looks bad," I said. "It will be bad," he replied. "No pucks days are usually killers."

Imlach walked into the rink and put on his skates. Wearing a dark blue windbreaker edged in Sabres gold and a baseball cap with "Sabres" embroidered in script, he skated to center ice and blew his whistle. Players gathered round and heard him say there would be no pucks, then lace them in an obscenity-filled tirade that a Marine drill sergeant would be proud of. Then he had us stand in rows from goal line out to blue line. It seemed only Dryden and me were free of hangovers.

"Okay, here's the deal. When I blow the whistle and point forward, you skate forward. When I blow the whistle again, you stop and skate in the direction I point. And so on. Everybody understand? We're gonna keep doing that until I say enough," Imlach called out with a glare.

The groans were audible. Stop-and-start drill skating is bad enough. But doing it in spurts in all four directions, with constant changes, is exhausting and just brutal. Even with breaks to catch one's breath, they are about as tiring as any drill in hockey. They are used almost exclusively as punishment. Punished we were. Imlach's whistle blew every four or five seconds. We skated back and forth to one side or another, with no pattern, and only a 15- to 30-second break every five minutes. Imlach needed to give some breaks as he didn't want to kill us all (at least, I don't think he did), just make us suffer. A half hour went by and my body was about ready to give up. Doing these drills is even worse for a goalie. We carried 30 to 40 pounds of equipment, including bulky leather and deer hair leg pads, once it was wet with perspiration and moisture from the ice. In addition, goalies prefer their skate edges a little dull so they can slide laterally more easily in the goal crease. This means stopping and starting takes more physical energy for goalies than other players, who keep sharp concaved edges on their skates.

Dryden and I were next to each other. He was my Gibraltar. He kept telling me during the breath-catching breaks to "Keep it up, big fella. You can make it."

"I'm the PR man, in his thirties, for God's sake," I wanted to shout back, "and I'm not a professional athlete; not in shape like you guys." But I couldn't get the words out, I was so out of breath. However, I persevered, and so did Dryden. The whistle kept blowing, and Imlach kept thrusting his arm in random directions.

Fallout began, as first Allan Hamilton headed to the boards and leaned over them to vomit. Two more of his teammates (and mates at Ace's) headed the same way for the same reason. Eddie Shack left the ice, muttering in his raspy way that Imlach was trying to kill us. The whistle kept blowing and the rest of us kept skating. Finally Imlach realized he was about to overdo it. The Sabres had a game in two nights, and exhausting the guys without hangovers would just reduce his chances of a win. "It's over," he shouted. "You can have pucks now." A trainer dumped a bag of practice pucks over the boards, but they just sat there in a black heap. There wasn't a player left with the energy to use them.

I could hardly walk the next day, but I had stuck it out. From that day on, for the next decade or so, I was treated well by each succeeding batch of players. The word got around that I wasn't a front-office spy and that I would hang in there with them. Besides, I was a morale builder in goal.

Chapter 8
Taro Lives and Other Conceits

"We're trying to encourage fans to identify with the Sabres, not hack them off. You and your goons are acting like censors...storm troopers. You don't even get half their signs, so you tear them down."

–Paul Wieland

The Phantom Sign Makers

Taro Tsujimoto was a morale builder among Sabres fans. His legend grew quickly because of the actions of a group of season-ticket holders who sat in the balcony in Memorial Auditorium and hung banners on the balcony face. They called themselves the "Phantom Sign Makers" and were clever with pithy signs that were at times more social commentary than hockey cheerleading.

They invented the "Taro Sez" motif and nearly every game hung a banner in which Taro said something funny and/or pertinent. We showed their work on home television broadcasts and talked about them on radio shows, inviting members of the sign-making crew to make interview appearances at times. Two of the ringleaders—Dave Hyzy and Steve Hill—keep in touch with me 30 years later, and they promise to bring Taro back to signs in the current Sabres arena if the team returns to wearing its traditional uniforms all the time.

Their signs were always funny and often irreverent. Mike Scanlan, an old fight manager who had been hired as the Sabres' security director by Dave Forman, didn't get the humor on some occasions. If he didn't understand what Taro was talking about, Scanlan would send some of his rent-a-cops over to tear down the banners. When this happened too often for my taste, and the Phantoms even complained about how hours of work were wasted when a sign was torn down, Mike and I had it out.

That's a kind way to describe our confrontation. Mike was a tough Irishman who had been in a tough business. His temper was hair-trigger, and mine was nearly a match. We would yell and scream at each other, and if we had been younger, I suspect we would have come to blows. "What the hell do you think you're doing?" I shouted. "We're trying to encourage fans to identify with the Sabres, not hack them off. You and your goons are acting like censors...storm troopers. You don't even get half their signs, so you tear them down."

Dave Forman would intercede in these loud arguments, and somehow he would calm the both of us down. Mike would then promise he would at least check with me before ripping down any more signs, and I would promise to talk to the Phantoms again to make sure they understood double entendre was not a good idea, no matter how funny it was.

The Phantoms and their Taro signs were noted by visiting newspapermen covering games from the press box high near the Aud rafters. Every time I was asked about Taro, I would keep a deadpan expression and explain that we still weren't sure whether Tsujimoto was ever going to show up. Technically, some kid named Tsujimoto could show up for training camp, and if one did, I'd be first to welcome him and hold a press conference.

Ted Darling and other members of the Sabres broadcast team would talk about Taro on the air occasionally, speculating about his skills and his future if he did come to camp. Darling was so revered by listeners and so respected for his straightforward coverage of the games that many listeners never doubted there was a Taro, or that he was Sabres property.

By the spring of 1976 Taro had become at least a minor part of the Sabres persona. After all, he was listed in the official NHL guide in the draft selections, so he was the real deal even as far as the league was concerned.

In the 1970s bumper stickers were in their heyday. This was the time when cars actually had bumpers, big wraparound pieces of chrome-coated steel, attached to the frame and prominent on the rear and back of each car. Some manufacturers were integrating bumpers into the car designs, but there was still plenty of space on most to display bumper stickers. They promoted commercial ventures, community causes, or even the local college and pro sports teams. Sometimes they were genuinely funny. Sometimes they were vulgar or just lame jokes. Every year the Sabres would produce a new bumper sticker that was mailed to all season-ticket holders along with playoff tickets. The Sabres missed the playoffs two years in a row at the beginning of the franchise, but a Stanley Cup Finals appearance in 1975 was the beginning of a long run by Buffalo that extended the season each spring.

Taro was a natural for the sticker the year after he was

drafted. We wanted one that would be an eye-catcher and would be mounted by fans on their cars, even fans who ordinarily didn't take to the idea. So we contacted the International Institute in Buffalo in search of a Japanese translator. Once found, the translator took the English phrase "Think Stanley" and turned it into Japanese characters. The bumper sticker design was ready in a day, with a Sabres logo to the left, the words "Taro Sez" in English next, and then the rest in Japanese, with a Stanley Cup to the far right.

The bumper sticker was a smash, though no one except those who could read Japanese was able to figure out what it said. We teased our ticket holders, not announcing the translation until a few days later.

Taro's reign as the Sabres' playoff symbol lasted only one year, as the Sabres were eliminated early. But his reign as one of the team's most notable draftees lasted until 2005, when the NHL finally figured out he really didn't exist and removed his name from the list of draftees in the official record book.

As recently as 2002, one of the bumper stickers was up for sale on eBay, with an opening bid price of $2. And there's still a hockey writer in a Buffalo newspaper who ends his column with a "Taro Says" segment.

Gare Arrives

Danny Gare came into the NHL with attitude and backed it up with talent. He was listed at a mere 5'9" and 175 pounds, but all of that was athletic with the heart and mind of a fierce competitor. He was drafted in 1974 after a brilliant junior career in Calgary. He related his experience at turning pro with the Sabres when the World Hockey Association was also trying to grab junior talent in Canada.

"I was also drafted from Calgary and the WHA. It was interesting. I was drafted by the Winnipeg Jets and I remember my agent at the time was Larry Sazant," Gare recalled. "He had a whirlwind tour through the Western Canadian League. I think what

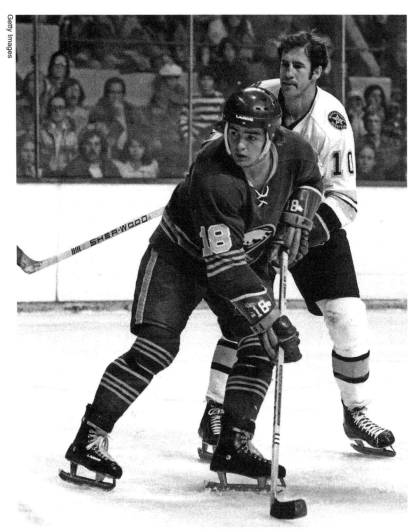

Danny Gare was a goal scorer and a feisty skater for the Sabres.

happened there was he talked with most of the WHA coaches and there were a few who probably offered kickbacks [to agents] if a player signed with a WHA team. You know I had three great years in Calgary. My last year I broke the record for the most goals, and I also broke the penalty minutes record. I think it was 268 all told.

"I know that was what my father wanted as my mentor [to be

a tough player]. A lot of what I became is because of the time he spent with me, and he pushed me in the right directions. I think the one thing I had to do was to be physically strong because I wasn't big and I had to have upper-body strength. I had to know how to fight, to box, and that was something I could do pretty well. That helped me in the draft, going in the second round, because that year there was an underage draft, and I remember a lot of players that got pushed back because the WHA went to an underage a few weeks prior to the NHL draft. I was [drafted] in the third round by Winnipeg [WHA]. Grant Fuhr, my roommate in junior at Calgary, called me up the night before the NHL draft and wished me luck. The next day, we [my dad, mom, and I] were at home in Nelson [British Columbia], and I really hoped I could get drafted so I could get a half decent contract. I remember listening to it on the radio, and Fuhr went in the seventh or eighth pick in the first round. I was shocked because they were starting to pick on under-age guys, and I remember calling Grant and congratulated him, and I still hadn't been drafted yet. I went 29th to the Sabres and was very happy about it. There were guys like Mike Rogers who I played junior with who had a great year with me in Calgary that didn't go until the fifth round.

"That was a shocker. I guess it was good, being drafted by both teams, or leagues I should say. There was some negotiation going on and Winnipeg wanted me real bad. The Sabres got wind of this. I knew what I wanted. I wanted to play in the NHL.

"My agent said, 'Let's wait and see what everyone will throw at you.' So what happened was we agreed on a five-year deal with the Sabres and had a pretty good signing bonus, and what happened was Punch still didn't believe I was going to sign with him so—God bless his soul—he flew all the way to Calgary. I'll never forget this was on a Sunday. It was Father's Day and he flew all the way out. I flew into Calgary and we signed the contract at the airport. That's how much he was committed to me. When I saw that, I felt that they really wanted me; it made me really want to play hard that summer to be prepared for training camp. It was funny because Punch flew right back to Toronto and Buffalo. He stayed for about an hour after that and I think we had lunch. It was a Sunday and I remember I think my signing bonus was $50,000, which was a lotta, lotta money back then. And I remember my mom saying, 'Don't lose the check, don't lose the check.' I put it in my pocket and flew home."

Gare Hit the Ice Running

Danny Gare remembers his first days with the Sabres: "I went to training camp in St. Catharines. I remember staying at the Holiday Inn. I will never forget it as long as I live. It's an impressionable time when you're a youngster, to go in and try to make an NHL team. I didn't know whether or not I was good enough, but I felt I was because I played with a lot of guys who moved on to the NHL. I played with Bobby Nystrom, with [Grant] Fuhr, and Jimmy Watson. And against a number of others who would make it to the NHL.

"One of the first guys I ran into in the hotel lobby was Brian Spencer. We had rookie camp at first, but Spinner [Spencer] came in early. I knew Spinner from Nelson, where he used to come up in the summers to work the hockey school there. It was good because Spinner was always upbeat. He said: 'You're going to have a good year,' which made me feel great. I had been watching the Sabres in Calgary when they went to the first round of the playoffs against Montreal. I was charged up by 'Thank You Sabres' when I got to see that on TV and CBC. Buffalo had Perreault, Martin, and Schony. I really thought, 'Wow.' I was just about to start with this team. Punch Imlach was a legend and he was someone I think everyone idolized when he was growing up, knowing about the Toronto Maple Leafs. I got to meet the Knox family and they were very, very supportive. When we had our training camp, and later when I got to know Dave Forman. Then I met [right winger] Larry Mickey—Mondello—we gave him that nickname because he had a round face like the character on *Leave It to Beaver*. Larry was a guy whose job I might take. Obviously I was there to take a job from someone and he was there battling and helping guys at rookie camp.

"I remember one time Schony was behind the net and he checked me. Then he comes down with this big paw and says, 'Welcome to the league.' I guess I was a bit awestruck when I saw Perreault and guys like that skating around in that little barn in St. Catharines. I'll never forget the first exhibition game I played. We took Allegheny Airlines along with the Cincinnati farm team into Philly. There was a Cincy game against the Philadelphia Firebirds first, as well as a Sabres-Flyers game, and we stayed in some little dump of a hotel, and I remember I couldn't sleep. I walked over to the rink where an American League game was under way. I can remember some of the guys in the game. Paul McIntosh and Michel Deziel, for sure.

"There was a big brawl as soon as I walked in the door. Everyone was in the fight, and I said, 'Here we go.' I guess that was part of my induction into the National Hockey League. When Craig Ramsay and I went out, they had won the Cup the year before and so they had all this big hullabaloo and it was jam-packed. Kate Smith was singing and all that stuff. You want to talk about just being thrown into a fire? And that was pretty much it. When we lined up against Schultz, Saleski, and Clarke, and Schultz was next to me, I remember running him into the end boards in the first shift; I was going to do anything I could do to make this team, and the crowd went 'Ooh.' When the puck came back, he went to the boards and I went back up the ice so close you could smell his breath. Then he jumped me and the ice cleared at about 35 seconds into the game. We had a brawl that went from one end to another.

"I could handle myself in fights, and I did all right and being the new kid on the block. Dave [Schultz] said, 'Hey, you little midget, what are you doing? Are you a tough guy?' That's how it started, and you know from there in camp they were great with me. The other part of it was I took Larry Mickey's job on the third line and Mondello played on the fourth line. But the nice part of all of that was through the years Larry always helped me out with players to watch for, like the way St. Louis's Barclay Plager would come across, and this goalie's weak on the side. He just gave me a little book on certain things. That was what the game was all about, what the dressing room was all about. We had some great individuals, like Roger Crozier. Then Freddie Stanfield came in later that year. He was a big part of the leadership. But the big thing was my first game and that was the one I really [remember]. I came back from St. Catharine's and the camp moved to the Aud."

View from the Top

Gare would make the Buffalo Auditorium a friendly home to his talents from his first shift in the NHL, but unlike many pros who never look much beyond the 200-by-85-foot ice surface, Gare was curious about what would be his workplace at least half the time.

"You look up in the stands and you see the gold, the red, and the blue seats all around. I remember after my first practice in the Aud, I went up to the oranges [seats]. I climbed all the way to the top and sat there on top of the heap. I was all by myself and I just wanted to get the feel of what it would be like for someone to watch me as I scored a goal or what it would be feeling like. And I'll never forget the feeling that it was so steep and so way over the top of the ice surface, and it seemed like a long way down," he said.

"The crowd at my first game against the Bruins made me more anxious to get out there and do well. I remember lining up for the national anthem. Joe Byron was the singer then. As he sang I was looking up into the oranges from the blue line and I thought, here I was, going up against Cashman and Hodge and Orr. It was just surreal. You were really there and you had all this around you, and it just happened so fast. What happened was I scored a goal in 18 seconds. It was awesome. I shot the puck around the boards and Rammer [Craig Ramsay] took a shot. I got the rebound and put it between Orr's legs into the goal. Orr was so mad he fired the puck out of the zone. He was so PO'ed. That was the moment I thought maybe I belonged in the league. It was certainly a great welcome for me.

"We did go on and play in the Finals, which were awesome. We had broken a record for points that year. I really loved the way

[Don] Luce and Ramsay played with me, and we really understood each other. That line I think the next year [was] when I scored the 50 goals. These guys were awesome; great checkers who really understood the game and defense. I tried to push the offense. We checked all the top lines, which we did, the Bossys and the Lafleurs. Whoever they were, they always wanted to leave the zone early, so I told Donnie and Rammer, 'Let's try and pin them down and let's try and react a little more and the offense will come.' Schony and Billy Hajt were smart enough to pinch it at the right times. The only bad part about it was I was always PO'ed when we had to kill penalties because I had to do more rotations on the bench. I was close to going on the ice and then if there was a penalty, guess what, I had to go all the way around and wait for my line's turn. Plus, I didn't play power play hockey in my first years because the [French] Connection was there."

Chapter 9
A Cup Final in Five Seasons

"Sometimes we would get fog in a rink where we were practicing, but I never recall it happening during an NHL game. You really couldn't see more than 30 or 40 feet at times. It must have been hell for the goalies."

–Danny Gare

The Flyers' Bobby Clarke fights off a Buffalo check during the infamous fog game.

The Infamous Fog Game

It was May 20, 1975, a day when freakish weather conditions brought midsummer heat to Buffalo, along with high humidity. The winter load of ice hadn't even cleared Lake Erie into the Niagara River, and Memorial Auditorium was located just 100 yards from the lake and the adjoining Buffalo River. Conditions were perfect for a sauna, not a hockey game.

The Sabres had slunk back into town after being pasted by the Flyers 4–1 in the first game of the Stanley Cup Finals, and then edged 2–1 in the second game. Buffalo was being outplayed, with Philadelphia's checkers and bully boy tactics working against a Sabres team that relied on speed and offensive fire power from the French Connection and emerging goal scorers on two other lines. Only Buffalo fans seemed optimistic about the series. The Sabres themselves were noncommittal, after beating their brains out trying to score on Bernie Parent.

At 4:00 PM, members of the Buffalo public relations staff climbed the 100-plus steps to the Aud press box, a steel-floored late addition to the Aud that was ready just before opening night in 1970. The press box hung from the building's rafters, tied into the roof by beams. It had a total of 50 seating positions, and they were too few to handle the requirements of television, radio, and print media for a Cup Final. Many journalists were actually required to sit in seats in the crowd, and the complaints had come fast and furious about this situation. In 1975, print journalists, mainly newspaper reporters, were the largest and most important media contingent covering the NHL. The Philistines of television were edging their way into the mix, their demands and space requirements increasing every year, every month, and every week.

The PR staff had gone up to the press box for a final check of all the required and requested phone lines, broadcast positions, and seat locations for the media. Everyone in that media horde wanted to sit closest to center ice. It was like the biblical story about the feast where the humble are exalted and the exalted are humbled. The newspaper gang couldn't sit at center ice because television needed a center-ice camera position in the press box. At least that's what the people from *Hockey Night in Canada* said. It was a weeknight game, so NBC wasn't on hand, but Ted Darling was doing the game for the local NBC affiliate. The Flyers also had a telecast, and there were three radio broadcasts. Fifty seats were just about enough for TV, radio, and the PR staff with the league's official scorekeeper and his assistant thrown in, too. It was a logistical nightmare at best, but it got worse quickly.

At 4:00 PM the temperature in the press box was 118 degrees on a wall thermometer mounted near the ramp entrance. There wasn't a breath of air in the building, just oppressive heat, and no way to cool it down. The Aud not only failed to have air conditioning, but its ventilation system was nonexistent as well. Most fresh air came from opening all the entrance doors, with a little added by some anemic built-in fans. The thermometer reading shocked the PR staff. How would anybody be able to stand it after 16,000-plus fans packed the building three hours later?

Sabres play-by-play man Rick Jeanneret and I were doing the local radio broadcast of the game that night, jammed into a small space and leaning forward over the counter rim of the press box to be able to see all the ice below. That was the only way to get the entire game in your field of vision, as the press box was so high and at such a steep angle to the ice. After a game broadcasters would complain of bellyaches and rib soreness from constantly leaning forward against the counter edge. Jeanneret is a hardy soul who's still broadcasting Sabres games 33 years later, and he was able to concentrate as long as he kept his parched throat lubricated with a suitable malt beverage. At 120-plus degrees by faceoff time, the supply line of malt beverages needed to be ample.

What he saw below was a wide-open game—the way the Sabres liked to play. The goals were coming fast, until the action ground to a halt for a reason that never has happened in an NHL game since, and likely never had happened before. Fog rolled in, not on little cat's paws, but like a cumulus cloud frosting a mountain top. By the middle of the first period the referee had seen enough, or not seen enough. At ice level there was so much fog at times that the goalie at one end, the Flyers' Bernie Parent, couldn't see his Buffalo counterpart in his crease at the other end of the ice. This would play a critical part much later in the game.

The play stopped with a faceoff to come in the Buffalo end. Four young men who worked on the ice when the Zamboni machine was cleaning between periods skated out waving white bath towels. Working in pairs and holding the towels tightly like sails between their extended arms, the men skated round and round, cupping bits of the fog in the towels and moving it around. They skated for about three minutes the first time out and managed to move some of the fog but really couldn't disperse it.

Not a one of them was a good skater, but then who could be when trying to keep a bath towel stretched to a partner, hanging on to two corners and scooping at a fog bank. It was a crazy, off-kilter ballet.

The game resumed for a minute or two, and the fog settled back in. Down on the ice the players were frustrated and worried. "Sometimes we would get fog in a rink where we were practicing," said Danny Gare. "But I never recall it happening during an NHL game. You really couldn't see more than 30 or 40 feet at times. It must have been hell for the goalies."

It was hell for both of them, and it was viewing hell for the fans sitting in the high-priced seats lower in the Aud bowl. Up in the press box Jeanneret and other broadcasters continued their game call as best as they could. But the game stopped several more times in that first period as the white stuff built up. With their bath towel fog sails, the skating rink attendants tried to move the white stuff away, with little success. Then someone got a better idea, and each team was asked to put all its players on the ice and skate rapid circles in its defensive zone. The crowd cheered when they saw the fog lift after the mass skates by the Flyers and the Sabres. The crowd wasn't happy for long.

As soon as play resumed, the fog would settle in, only pierced when a winger trailing a white vapor would rush up the ice, the fog closing in behind him as he moved from zone to zone. Both teams came out for the fog-attacking circles on skates time after time, and the time on the clock crept along. With 16,000 fans in a closed arena, it only got hotter. Some fans were faint. A few fainted.

Regulation time ended with the score tied at 4. Overtime began with the Flyers' Parent defending the net at the end of the ice that seemed to have more fog problems. Out of the fog came the French Connection—Perreault, Martin, and Robert. They hit the Flyers blue line in full flight, with Perreault sliding a hard pass to Robert on his right. The crack of the puck leaving Robert's stick could be heard, but Parent couldn't see the puck leave because of the fog, and Robert's shot beat him on the short side to end the game.

Parent never used the fog as an excuse for not stopping the shot, but ice-level film of the play showed him leaning forward in his crouch, eyes scanning the fog for the puck he couldn't see on the stick he hardly saw. Thousands of the fans in the Aud only knew there was a goal when they saw the red light go on. That night, despite the fog, they went home hot and happy. Since that night nothing like that fog has crept into an NHL arena—on little cats' paws or otherwise.

Batman

Jim Lorentz made a bit of sports history during the same Stanley Cup series against the Flyers, in the same building. With a flick of his stick he killed a flying creature in front of 16,433 Buffalo fans and a television audience.

"I suppose I can claim it will never happen again," he recalled. "The bat had been dive-bombing the crowd. Maybe somebody brought it in and let it loose. I don't know how it got in there. It was a distraction, without a doubt, not only for the crowd but for the players, because it often came down near the ice.

"I can remember several occasions when it came close enough that [Bernie] Parent was swinging at it with his goal stick and missing it. My memory is that was the only thing he missed in the series. I was waiting for a faceoff in the Flyers zone. I looked down the ice toward our net, and I saw the bat coming toward me. At this time, deep into the game, the bat didn't have much energy. It was flying in a straight line, and flying high enough that I was able to get at it. I just reached up and swatted it out of the air, and it fell to the ice. And everyone that was on the ice at the time looked at each other. 'Okay, what do we do now?' The officials didn't want any part of the bat.

"Rick MacLeish [of the Flyers] had been waiting to take the faceoff against me. He took off his glove, picked it up, and buried the bat in the penalty box. There were—so I'm told—hundreds of calls to *Hockey Night in Canada*. People wanted to have me arrested for cruelty to animals. I got letters from all over the United

Jim Lorentz (left) on the road with Gerry Desjardins (center) and Jim Schoenfeld (right).

States and Canada asking me if I felt more like a man for killing a bat. I always said that I'd like to take all these people that objected, put them in a room, and let a bat loose and see what they'd do.

"The only regret I have is that when the bat was laying on the ice, I should have shot it in the net past Bernie. Maybe that would have changed our luck.

"There's a sidebar to this. I'm a big Yankees fan. I went to a game in Toronto in the old Exhibition Stadium the day of the Dave Winfield incident. I actually saw him intentionally throw the ball at the seagull. He caught the seagull in the head, and one of the attendants ran out from the dugout with a towel, covered the bird, and took him off the field. The next day I received several calls from Toronto reporters who were comparing the two incidents.... I was at that game, I said, and the only difference is that Winfield was arrested and I wasn't."

Lorentz was discouraged at what came next in ensuing seasons. "I guess we just weren't good enough to win the Stanley Cup, and I felt if the management had made a few more moves— perhaps bringing in a little more muscle—we might have won the Stanley Cup the next year or the year after.... Unfortunately for us, and for the rest of the NHL, the Islanders were building a dynasty. The next year we ended up losing to them. I don't know if I was bitter at the end of my career in Buffalo, but I felt that they were playing players that weren't as good as some of the players they were sitting. That didn't sit too well with me. One of the reasons I retired is that I felt that [if] this was the way the business was going to operate, I didn't want to continue. If you're not going to play your best guys and give yourself the best chance to win, then that's not the way you operate a franchise or any business."

"Tickets"

The bachelor Gare shared a house with teammates Derek Smith and Terry Martin. The trio insisted they take turns cooking, but there weren't any gourmet chefs in the making. Instead, they were highly visible to young women in the Buffalo metropolitan area. It wouldn't be fair to say that they were living life in some kind of fast lane—they were hockey players first—but they had the kind of fun that young bachelors did then and do today. Gare was the most voluble and the most energetic in his quest for new friends, nearly all female. That led him to the nickname he carries to this day, as a TV broadcaster for the Columbus Blue Jackets. He's called Tickets, and it represents his seemingly eternal quest for more tickets for any given home or road game involving the Sabres.

Jim Schoenfeld recalls Gare in action: "He would meet girls in a bar and he'd always promise them tickets for the game coming up. Sometimes he'd forget that he promised them, and the girls would show up at the box office to pick them up. Then the call would come down to the dressing room, and Danny would be frantic. He'd rush from one player to another asking if he could buy their tickets for the game. He'd yell, 'Tickets, I need tickets,' and soon that's what we called him. He still has the name, 30 years later."

The Buffalo Herders

Seymour Knox's idiosyncrasies were almost charming. He wore medium gray or dark suits, every inch the businessman. But he was totally unconscious of the appearance of his clothes, and he wore the same tatty tan raglan-sleeved raincoat for the first seven years I worked for him. He combined that with a ratty fedora. Both belonged on the "throw out" pile in a charity clothing outlet. Once he was asked why he was wearing a shirt that had obviously received plastic surgery, with new sleeves added after the elbows on the original had worn out. He replied that no one would notice, as he always kept his suit coat on outside of the office. But he never minded being kidded about his lack of sartorial splendor. It was traditional at the annual players' and staff Christmas skating party for the team captain to give each Knox a gift. One year when the devilish Danny Gare was captain, he presented Seymour a new raincoat and hat, pleading with him to throw the old ones out immediately. Seymour threw them out as far as we know (or maybe just wore them on weekends) and laughed the loudest at being razzed by the gift.

Seymour didn't like firing anyone, but it was his job to tie the can to a few general managers along the way. In the end, Punch Imlach was dismissed because he booked Memorial Auditorium himself for a certain night in the winter of 1979. Seymour had told his fellow owners that the Sabres would host a traveling Soviet team that night in Buffalo, part of a North American road tour that brought extra bucks into owners' and league coffers. Punch was against playing the Soviets once more, as Buffalo had never lost a game to various teams from behind the Iron Curtain in years previous. "What do we have to prove?" he shouted at Seymour one day as we three sat in his office. "We're not playing that game. And that's that." Seymour visibly reddened and said, "We'll see about that." He forcefully ordered Punch to play the game, and Imlach replied, "We'll see about that."

Poor Dave Forman, the club's administrative vice president. It was his job to contact the city on orders from Seymour and book the Aud for the night in question. When he did so—or tried to—he was told it was already rented. "By whom?" he asked, and was told by George Imlach, who had paid cash up front. That was the final straw for Seymour. The team had not been performing well, but it was Punch's intransigence that cost him his job. A few more days and several more losses, and Knox pulled the trigger. A news release announcing Imlach's firing was written, including the dismissal of Coach Marcel Pronovost, seemingly caught in the middle on this one. Soon the phone rang in Imlach's office. It was Seymour, asking Punch to meet with him. "That's it, boys," he said. "I'm getting bleeping fired." He went upstairs to Seymour's office and was only there a few minutes before returning. Punch was swearing in rapid fire.

He called in Pronovost, scouting director John Andersen, and me. Punch ranted about the unfairness of it all, but he never referred to his Aud booking that had been a direct defiance of Seymour's wishes. Punch told Pronovost and Andersen how they should handle things for the rest of the season and asked me to give them both special care. Soon Pronovost was called on the phone, and he left, expecting to meet with Seymour about the parameters of Sabres life without Imlach. He came downstairs ashen and unemployed. I had known he was also going to be canned but was under orders not to tell Marcel or anybody else.

Once a firing was done, Seymour seldom mentioned it, except to praise the former employee for the good things he or she had done. For example, when he fired Scotty Bowman many years later, dumping another Hall of Fame coach out the door, Seymour phoned the PR staff early that morning and told us what was coming. "When you come in the office, tell Scotty I want him upstairs right away. Make sure he knows that 'right away' means right away." Scotty was the second famous GM/coach that Seymour fired, yet strangely, both got over it quickly. In fact, Imlach had a warm relationship with Knox until his death, and would come back on occasion to visit his friends at the Sabres offices.

Norty Knox, for his part, stayed on the outside for most of the early years. He deferred to his brother in operational matters, and he didn't even have an office in the Sabres complex. It was at board meetings with other investors that his financial knowledge came more into play. Norty was always supportive of the people who made the Sabres tick, the front-office staff. He wandered among their desks regularly, chatting with everyone, and occasionally would tell everyone to go home an hour or two early on a warm summer day.

Roger the Dodger

Tom Webster, who'd played his junior hockey in Niagara Falls, Ontario, is part of Buffalo Sabres history in a backhanded way. It was Webster who was drafted by Imlach with his first choice in the expansion selection in June of 1970. The NHL was upping its teams to 14, with Buffalo and Vancouver getting the chance to take players unwanted by the league's other 12 teams. Webster had been in the Boston Bruins farm system since coming south from far-off Kirkland Lake, Ontario. Though he was a gifted minor league scorer, Webster wasn't what Imlach had in mind when the coach took him with his first choice.

Sid Abel, then the general manager of the Detroit Red Wings, had an eye on Webster, but he had no direct way of obtaining him because Webster was on the expansion draft list available only to Buffalo and Vancouver. Imlach knew that solid goaltending could save his yet-to-be-named expansion roster in many game situations. He needed a goalie who could steal games if there was any way to steal them, but better yet, entertain the home fans with his skills under all circumstances. That man was Detroit's Roger Crozier, a slight native of Bracebridge, Ontario, north of Toronto. Crozier was so good in his prime that he won the Conn Smythe Trophy as the most valuable player in the Stanley Cup playoffs in 1966, even though he played with the losing Detroit team in the Finals. Crozier couldn't have been more than 5'7" tall, though he was always listed at 5'8", and he didn't top the 140-pound mark until he was in his thirties. He was beyond nimble in the net, the first NHL goalie you could describe as bouncing around in the net like a rubber ball.

Today's goalies spend more time on their knees than a cloistered nun, but Roger could get up and down...and up again...better than anyone who had played the game to that time. That made Roger an anomaly, as the best goalies of the time played the position standing up as long as they could, cutting angles down on shooters by moving out from the goal crease.

There are reasons for the differences between goalies then and now. In 1970, a professional goaltender wore equipment that weighed 30 pounds or more when it was dry. It didn't stay dry for long. The leg pads were stuffed with deer hair and covered with custom-sewn leather, equipment that became sodden in a steam bath arena under bright lights. When a goalie went down in the process of making a save, he had to drag those heavy leg pads to get back up again. Today goalies wear leg pads made of synthetic materials that weigh half as much, plus they don't pick up moisture during play. All goalie equipment is lighter and more flexible, which allows current goalies to play a different style, with most on their knees, fanning their goal pads toward each goal post. When Crozier played, he combined today's style (before it had evolved) with the traditional stand-up method. Roger would do just about anything to make a save, including hanging off the goal's metal crossbar. He really didn't have a weak spot as a goalie, or a fault to be analyzed by a goalie coach. First of all, there weren't any goalie coaches in 1970, so every goalie had to work out his style on his own. No one was quite sure what a goalie should do to stop the puck, except pattern his style on someone else who was good at the job.

"I never had any technical coaching," Crozier said. "I had to work it out by myself from the time I was a kid."

Crozier played his junior hockey in St. Catharines, the training camp site of the Sabres for more than a decade. As a junior, he starred for the OHA Teepees, leading them to a national junior championship, the Memorial Cup. He was a familiar figure in Buffalo's Memorial Auditorium in the late 1950s and early 1960s while he was in juniors, hired to serve as the backup goalie for both teams when the American League Buffalo Bisons played a home game. Those were the days when professional teams—including the NHL—only carried one goaltender. If a goalie was cut or hurt during a game he either was patched up and returned to play or the game was held up until a backup could be found. Sometimes the backup was a team trainer who had some experience as an amateur goalie. The late Lefty Wilson, longtime trainer of the Red Wings, was one of those old goalies, and he actually played in NHL games for Detroit, Toronto, and Boston when injuries put the starter for those teams out of action.

The Buffalo Bisons were the high minor pro affiliate of the Chicago Blackhawks, and the Hawks' junior team was Crozier's Teepees. On backup duty, 18-year-old Roger sat nervously at the end of the simple press row in Buffalo, twitching and swallowing hard as the game unfolded in front of him. He always appeared nervous on the ice, too, and it wasn't until he adopted a mask that the nervousness didn't show. He turned pro in 1962 and a year later was dealt to Detroit, where in 1964–65 he started 70 games with 40 wins and six shutouts. For that achievement he was voted winner of the Calder Memorial Trophy as the NHL Rookie of the Year.

Crozier's achievements came at a cost to his health. He was diagnosed with pancreatitis, a disease that made it difficult to eat properly and to keep up his strength and weight. By the time Imlach had a shot at Crozier, the Red Wings had given up on him, largely because his illness kept him sidelined often. Imlach was willing to take a chance on Roger. Punch was cagey, but he was a gambler at heart. Crozier was a gamble that paid off for Buffalo from opening night at home in October of 1970. Roger startled the Buffalo crowd with 50 saves against Stanley Cup champion Montreal, keeping the new Sabres in the game as he flew hither and yon around the goal crease, stopping point-blank chances by the Canadiens. The final score was 3–0, with Montreal on top. However, Crozier had captured the fans in Buffalo, who were to see that kind of goaltending for seven seasons.

Roger often was a sick man. Because of his chronic illness, he was let off from practice the day after he played in a game, and soon Imlach would grant a practice day off to Crozier on any occasion that Roger asked for one. Even at practice, Roger was usually supported by an amateur goalie who took the majority of the workload while Roger lay face up on a players bench, his goalie gloves in use as a pillow.

He managed to keep the first-year Sabres respectable, flinging his wispy frame in front of the best shooters in the NHL. Buffalo finished that first year with the best record of any nonplayoff team, largely due to Crozier and Perreault. The next season, 1971–72, Roger faced a team-record 2,190 shots, about 30 a game, but his health remained precarious.

"I don't understand why anyone would want to be a goalie," he told me on more than one occasion. "You have to be nuts to do this job."

Crozier was able to play until 1977, with one of the highlights in his later career coming in the 1975 Stanley Cup Finals against Philadelphia. His illness made it impossible for him to play every game in the series, but when he played, the Sabres won, extending the series to a six-game Flyers victory.

Crozier was traded to Washington in 1977 and retired after

three games with the Caps. He became GM of the Caps for a short while when Max McNab was fired, before leaving hockey to join MBNA Bank, in Wilmington, Delaware.

Though he lacked a high school diploma, Crozier advanced quickly in the bank's administration, heading up facilities design for the massive credit card bank on its new campus. The roads and the pathways on the campus soon had hockey names: the Red Line, the Blue Line, and so forth.

Ironically, pancreatitis wasn't the enemy that killed Crozier in 1996. He died of cancer on January 11 of that year, and today he is honored by the NHL with the Roger Crozier Saving Grace Award. It goes to the goalie with the best save percentage during the season.

Chapter 10
The Dressing Room

"We have to go on the road again...to Van-bleeping-couver."

−Frank "Frankie" Christie

Frank Christie, the Sabres' first trainer, with coach Floyd Smith.

Fast Frankie

Quicksilver, it is called, the mercury inside a thermometer that would be impossible to capture once the glass tube that held it was broken.

Quicksilver, impossible to grasp, impossible to contain, impossible to measure.

The word *mercurial* comes from this, and the mythical Mercury, a Greek deity who moved at hyperspeed, doing the things that fast-acting gods do. Mercurial, quicksilver, fast-acting, and faster-talking Frank Christie was the Sabres' trainer from the day the team began operations, with a persona impossible to capture. Photographing Frankie wouldn't result in a clouded negative, a standard for ghost stories and spooky tales, but it probably wouldn't find Christie in the frame, as he always moved on to something else before he stopped long enough to pose. Christie was never still, and that wasn't the mark of just Christie, but of all hockey trainers. It's an inherited trait, not through blood lines but through necessity.

Hockey trainers begin and end their long days in the fetid air of a team dressing room, with the chance that the end of one day rolls right into the beginning of the next, particularly during the mix of road trip and home games in today's compressed game schedules, when a team might play four games in five nights in three different cities across North America.

In the days when Frankie broke into hockey, the air travel and compressed schedule didn't exist, but that didn't make the job any easier. Trainers weren't really trainers at all, at least not in today's professional sense. They weren't athletic trainers, with degrees in physical education or more, and backgrounds in physiotherapy, first aid, nutrition, and all. In Frankie's day, before World War II, they were usually young men who latched onto a hockey team as a kid, hanging out at the rink, volunteering to slog dirty laundry, pick up equipment, or just be a gofer for the team.

Frankie was a city kid from New York, not a hockey player. Many of his trainer friends were players of sorts, usually goaltenders who weren't quite good enough to be a regular on the team, but they combined that goaltending skill with the duties of a trainer to stay close to the game and make a very modest living.

Frankie is The Man

There were only a few training jobs in hockey when Frankie got his first as a stick boy for the old New York Americans before the war broke out. A stick boy is a sort of apprentice trainer. Sometimes they get a salary during the season, but they are rarely on the payroll all year round. Most of the time, stick boys are paid in cash. The money comes from the trainer's pocket stash that's one of the true slush funds in professional sport.

Work hard enough as a stick boy, sort out enough dirty laundry, hang up enough stinking equipment at 3:00 in the morning after the team arrives back from a road game in an arena 800 miles away, and you just might get a chance to move on to become a trainer. That's the way the system worked before World War II and through the first expansion of the NHL in 1967.

Frank Christie was never there when you wanted him. He was always an integral part of the Sabres, but impossible to place in any physical context. He moved every few seconds, even on a chair on a phone; he moved and bounced; bobbed and weaved.

He never seemed to stand still long enough to get into visual focus, and he spoke in sentence fragments, often interrupting himself with new thoughts, new phrases, and new dispositions in a stream of consciousness punctuated by the saltiest vocabulary imaginable. I am not sure Frankie even knew how salty he was. Professional sports in general, and hockey in particular, have a speech code that uses one Anglo-Saxon term for sexual congress as noun, pronoun, verb, adjective, adverb, preposition, punctuation mark, and even as part of a word.

Thus: "We have to go on the road again...to Van-bleeping-couver."

Frankie's language was vulgar and profane, and occasionally blasphemous, but it flowed from him naturally, and it couldn't mask his inherent flakiness. After a while you didn't notice the nasty words, just the syntax, which sometimes would leave a listener totally baffled.

There were times that we heard Frankie cover three or four topics in the same sentence in the same breath, and yet we couldn't understand what he meant at all. He wasn't the best at names, either, so he used "Whojamacallit" as an all-purpose proper name, substituting for the right one in nearly every circumstance. This led to sentences from Christie such as: "Whojamacallit called before, looking for you. He says Whojamacallit in Boston needs a Whatjamacallit for this weekend. So call him back."

"Do you have a number?" might be the tentative and hopeless rejoinder.

"No, but Whojamacallit has it. Ask him."

Christie would anger if any of us didn't understand him when he went off like this. And he went off like this nearly every waking moment. "What'sa matter with you?" he would challenge. "Don't you understand bleeping English?"

Christie was about 5'6" tall, with a wiry leathery body that only got a bit thicker as the years went by. He never seemed to work out, despite the availability of all the fitness equipment, and he never seemed to eat anything more than a sandwich, gobbled down between "Whojamacallits" and arguments with the players. The mercurial Christie doesn't rate the adjective only because he moved and talked fast. He would blow his stack as regularly as Old Faithful, screaming at everyone whenever he felt crossed. Sabres players (at least some of them) delighted in getting him to explode. When it happened, it was alarming. His face would turn beet red, his eyes would bulge behind his glasses, and a Vesuvius of curse words would erupt. The easiest way to set him off was to accuse him of stealing from the club, the unofficial way for trainers to make a living before the days of expansion, more jobs, and better salaries.

When Christie broke in, trainers might get $50 a week if they were really lucky, with no benefits or pensions, and 100-hour weeks to go along with the job. They were expected to augment their incomes through deals. Sometimes it was as simple as perks from an equipment supplier to the team, who did favors for the trainer by throwing in extra stuff to be sold in the gray market. Sometimes it was cash, as trainers were also the road secretaries for many teams, and since hockey teams and players weren't exactly welcome guests at many hotels, the payoff was in cash for room accounts. A trainer/road secretary could turn in one quote to team management and pay a lower number when settling out the hotel bill. The difference was cash in hand.

There were many ways to maneuver before the days of credit cards and direct billing, and some trainers learned them. They had to in order to make a living, and the finagling was by and large accept-able to the teams' managements as it kept actual salaries low.

Frankie always carried his pocket money in a cash roll, which often was so large it would bulge his pants pocket. Players would accuse him of wrapping two or three large denominations around the outside and filling the rest with singles. Infuriated, Christie would start peeling off fifties and hundreds one after another. I never saw anyone carry more cash in a roll, unless he still had one up on us all by using some counterfeit stuff.

Frankie had admirable strengths, loyalty and longtime friend-ships among them. His wife, Ruthie, turned him into a pussycat with her presence, and their home was a true cathedral of hockey. Their modest-sized downstairs recreation room was literally filled from ceiling to floor with souvenirs of the sport and memorabilia from other pro leagues in football, baseball, and basketball.

Frankie and Ruthie had one of everything there. If there ever was an object that could be construed as a souvenir or keepsake in the world of hockey, they had at least one in that McGee's closet of the room. Memorabilia from seat cushions to bats to banners to caps; from the clever to the hideous, the gallant to the gauche, crammed that room. There was nowhere to sit down, and few places to even stand, on the tour, a tour Frankie only gave to a select few.

With no children of their own, the Christies lived and breathed first the AHL Bisons and later the Sabres. Ruthie was a ticket office staffer with both franchises, but she and her husband seldom saw each other on the job except in passing. Compared to the skyrocket personality of her husband, Ruthie was placid. It is said that in their private moments, she could scald Frankie with ease. That's what marriage brings to even the most mercurial.

The Rumor Maker

As Christie's years with the Sabres approached a decade, some health problems arose, and he became what euphemistically was called "head trainer." This reduced the amount of physical work he needed to do, and it gave him a chance to play boss with a training staff. It also put him on the payroll, year-round. He was assigned to an office among the suits of the Sabres administration complex, up front in the Aud behind the ticket windows. Every day all summer long Frankie would show up for work and sit at his desk for several hours making phone calls to points across North America to exchange hockey gossip.

For if there was one job requirement of being a trainer in Chistie's days, it wasn't the ability to train but the ability to gossip. The best of the old-time trainers knew more about the sport, its players, its heroes and its bums, its machinations, and its misses than all the owners and coaches and general managers combined. They did it by exchanging every scrap of information every waking hour. They did it by the machine-gun approach, seldom evaluating the information, but always passing it on, trusting that the good stuff will rise to the top.

Every day Frankie would hang the phone from his ear, lean his elbows on his desk, and wriggle with anger or delight as he talked to his fellow trainers, players, and coaches scattered for their summers from Prince Rupert, British Columbia, to Noranda, Quebec. It didn't make any difference what they talked about, as long as there was grist for the rumor mill. Sometimes Frankie would forget that he was the original source of a rumor, and later announce that he had heard the rumor from someone somewhere else, and that gave it validity all its own. I tested this theory one day by giving Frankie a totally specious story about a player whom we both knew. I deliberately didn't make the story too notorious. In fact, it was essentially harmless, for I knew it would travel coast to coast in a matter of 24 hours. It traveled even faster. The best part was when Frankie came to me in my office after a day had passed and told me the whole rumor story, explaining how he had heard it from a "friend in Toronto." He had completely forgotten I was the one who told him in the first place.

Christie never forgot his friends. Or his enemies. And if you could pin him down long enough he was inherently kind and loyal. But just as the mercury sliding from a broken thermometer, you could never pin him down.

Don Luce recalls that Christie and the others on the training staff were as much a part of the team as the players. "They were in the same family back then," he said. "They were our friends and we respected them because they cared about us—and about each other."

Rick Martin was Christie's nemesis, but all in good humor. "Rico used to drive Frankie crazy with one particular gag," said Jim Schoenfeld. "Frankie loved to talk on the phone. I mean he was always on the phone; sometimes he faked being on the phone so he didn't have to put up with us. So Rico would take some of the hot stuff—the hot salve that we would use on aching muscles and so forth—and put a coating on the phone hand set in the trainers' room. Then he'd go call the number and Frankie would answer, and put the hand set to his ear. Or Rico wouldn't even phone. He'd just wait until Frankie got a call. Frankie would get a really hot ear either way."

Porky

Then there was Encil "Porky" Palmer, whose nickname accurately describes a very round, very strong man. Porky was a very good amateur goalie in western New York despite his lifelong girth. He had two passions, hockey and baseball, a man for two seasons, with the winter game providing him a part-time job as an assistant to Christie.

Porky had two things that made him an above-average amateur goalie: a quick glove hand and supreme confidence. As a teenager he began hanging around the dressing room of the Buffalo Bisons, the American Hockey League precursor to the NHL Sabres. Christie had the Bisons trainer job, and Palmer was one of the kids Frankie would use for the slog jobs that exist around a hockey team.

Porky never was paid much, but as the stick boy, he was the ultimate source of good hockey lumber for generations of amateur players in the area. A trip to Porky's basement was a little bit of heaven to the amateurs, with bargain prices on sticks made for the pros. In the late 1960s Buffalo had a very competitive franchise in the AHL, and rivalry games between the Bisons and the Rochester Americans 70 miles east along the New York State Thruway were highlights of the regular season.

Buffalo's goalie was Eddie Chadwick (who later served as a Sabres scout). The Bisons were scheduled to play the Amerks in the War Memorial Arena in Rochester and Chadwick was to start. It was pretty much required, as the team only carried one goalie. But an injury in the warm-up left the Bisons with a problem. They needed a goalie.

Sometimes there wasn't one available. The Bisons once played an entire game with a forward named Orland Kurtenbach in the net. Buffalo won the game, which led many of his team-mates to suggest the aforementioned Kurtenbach, who never scored much as a winger, change his occupation to goalie.

In Rochester Punch Imlach had assembled a league power coached by Joe Crozier. Five years later Crozier led the young Sabres into their first Stanley Cup playoffs. But that night he was behind the Rochester bench, his team loaded with talent, some of it legitimate NHL talent. That's because Imlach, the general manager and coach in Toronto, took every advantage of the rules in force at the time. Players who displeased the boss in any NHL setting could be sent down to the minors on a yo-yo circuit. Punch particularly liked to discipline his Leafs and put fear into them by occasionally assigning even his first liners to do some time in

Rochester, and get a minor league paycheck to boot. Thus it was that the Crozier-led Amerks had Eddie Shack and Jimmy Pappin in their lineup, and a roster strong enough to win the AHL's Calder Cup as playoff champions the following spring.

While Buffalo goalie Chadwick writhed in the dressing room with a pulled groin that meant he could hardly walk, let alone skate, Porky Palmer fulfilled the dream of every stick boy. He put on Chadwick's equipment and took the ice with a mediocre Buffalo team against the best team in hockey outside of the NHL. When it was over there wasn't quite a storybook ending. The Amerks were just too good for the Bisons, and they won the game, 4–2. But Palmer was probably the best player in the game for Buffalo that night, facing 38 shots and keeping the Bisons competitive to the end. Later he worked as a trainer/second goalie in the old Eastern League and played more games at a lower level, but that night the stick boy who just decided to ride down to Rochester to help out Christie became a part of Buffalo hockey history.

Chapter 11
Too Much Time on Their Hands

"We had some good laughs with him. Scotty is a pretty serious guy, but he's a real fun guy as well, and he likes to have fun in the game."

–Mike Foligno

A Road Prank

Jokes didn't always happen in the dressing room. Bill Hajt recalled a trip west that had an unusual dessert course: "Scotty [Bowman] was coaching. I hadn't been playing well and had been benched for a few games. I was down in the dumps. Then Scotty took the whole team out to dinner at this nice big Denver prime rib place. It was the day after my 30th birthday and the day before John Van Boxmeer's, who had been traded to us. All of a sudden, the guys said, 'Hey, Bill and John, come here.' They put chairs in the front of the restaurant for us. And told us to sit in them.

"We knew something was up for sure. Then a girl came down the stairs in front of us. She was wearing a big fur coat. I took a little peek behind me and the whole restaurant had stopped. A crowd had accumulated about 10 feet behind. It was packed full of people, watching us and the girl in the fur coat. She came toward John and me, and she was carrying birthday party hats and those horns that you blow at a party. She handed them to us and said: 'Bill and John, if you're horny then blow your horn.' We started to blow our horns, and we knew this was going to be good. Then she started singing: 'Happy birthday to you.' She opened up her coat. Nothing on. Then she closed it and sang 'Happy birthday to you.' Opened it up again, and so on through the end of the song. Then handed out her business card. I think it said 'Strip Again.' So this was our birthday present.

"Now, the end of the story. Scotty dressed me the next night and the party joke must have had the needed effect on my play because we beat Colorado 4–3 and I had a goal and an assist and I was first star of the game."

Joe's Off to Jail

For reasons unexplainable, Buffalo cops of all sorts liked to befriend members of the Sabres in the 1970s. It may have been that so many used their badges to get free access to the sold-out Aud for Sabres games that they became died-in-the-wool fans. Or it may have been that they were so used to making traffic arrests of Sabres players that the police officers built up personal relationships. It's most likely that they were fans just like everyone else, but could get close to the players by merely flashing a badge or showing up in uniform.

For whatever reasons, there always seemed to be a Buffalo cop or two at every Sabres practice in the Aud. They were like wallpaper.

In 1976, the Sabres didn't have a first-round pick in the amateur draft and had to choose 33rd overall in what was considered a thin draft after the first few selections.

Buffalo took left winger Joe Kowal from the Hamilton FinCups of the OHA, a player that Imlach described as a big project, with the "big" meaning his size as well as how much work Joe would need. Kowal was 6'5" and well over 200 pounds, with very limited scoring skills, even as a junior. In a preseason game in Buffalo, Kowal had a great chance to score from about 10 feet in front of the net, and he fired his shot with the idea of putting it under the crossbar. He raised his arms in the classic celebration of a goal scored, but he wasn't that lucky. In trying to roof the puck he sent it over the glass and up two seating levels in the Aud, a good 30 feet higher than the top of the goal net.

Nonetheless, he was brought to Buffalo for some games in his first pro season, and he immediately insinuated himself in the dressing room the wrong way.

Kowal had had brushes with the law in his teens in Canada and was wont to brag about what a tough guy he was and how he stood up to the police officers who came into his life off and on. Rookies in the NHL were to be seen and not heard, particularly on a veteran team like the Sabres. But Kowal was free-spirited and was oblivious to the fact that his penchant for storytelling that portrayed himself as some tough-guy hero was extremely annoying to many of his new teammates.

One day, he came off the ice after practice, stripped off his jersey, dropped his gloves and stick, and was unlacing his skates when two uniformed Buffalo police officers walked into the dressing room. Everyone else knew what was going to happen next.

"Kowal, you're under arrest," said one cop. The other told Joe he'd have to come with them "right now." Joe blanched.

"What do you want me for?" he pleaded. "I ain't done nothing." The first cop said: "Just come along. You can explain it to the judge."

Joe had been bragging of how he had eluded Canadian authorities before, but he was a whiter shade of pale when the second cop snapped a set of handcuffs on his wrists. "Is this something from home [Canada]?" he asked. "Can't I at least get dressed?"

The officers grabbed the big rookie by each arm and marched him out of the dressing room. The players in the room had watched the whole thing in near silence, and they stayed quiet for about 30 seconds before the laughter began. It had all been a ruse, set up with two of their cop friends. Meanwhile, Kowal had been hustled out of the Aud and into the back of a Buffalo patrol car. He kept shouting he hadn't done anything, and the cops told him to shut up and take it like a man. They drove Joe around for a few minutes before returning to the Aud and confessing it all had been a joke.

A shaken Kowal walked back into the dressing room, swearing softly, but too mixed up to know what to do. He must have been mad as hell. But he must have been glad as hell that it was all a joke.

He never bragged about his law-baiting ways again. He also never found out who had arranged the joke. As the story goes, this one was a team effort.

What's Funny May Be in the Eye of the Beholder

When Scotty Bowman coached in the NHL, he had the reputation of being a stern taskmaster, and sometimes his players were in awe of the intensity of his personality. Scotty wasn't one to be fooled around with, or so some of his players thought. Mike Foligno, who played most of his career under Bowman, had a different take.

"There's some things that happened through the years, stories that you have to retell, that you just laugh about," he recalled. "One that comes to mind had a lot to do with Scotty. We had some good

Scotty Bowman was an intense coach—and a big winner.

laughs with him. Scotty is a pretty serious guy, but he's a real fun guy as well, and he likes to have fun in the game. But it's a very tough game because it's a business and he had a job to do.

"I'll never forget we were in Hartford and Scotty was walking out on the ice after the second intermission. He had to walk across the zone diagonally to get to the bench. Now as coach, if you have to walk across the ice diagonally, you better keep your head up for the players who are warming up. Sometimes they're looking over their shoulder, explaining a play or something. So as Scotty was walking across one night—he always had about 30 pens in his shirt pocket—Lindy Ruff was skating and talking with someone and didn't see Scotty. He ran into Scotty in front of thousands of people. Scotty was knocked on his rear end. Lindy fell over too, and he looked up and said, 'What the hell was that?' Then he looked over and saw Scotty lying on the ice. You never saw a guy with a face of panic so bad as Lindy. He got up and there were Scotty's pens all over the place. Scotty's tie was over to one side and his jacket opened up while he's scrambling to get up. Lindy was just panicking and he figured he might have seen his last game with the Buffalo Sabres for hitting the coach. He was so apologetic, helping to pick up the pens and helping to guide Scotty to his feet. Scotty wasn't hurt on the play and we had a few good laughs about it, but not Lindy. He was so embarrassed."

Walter Mitty on Skates

One evening in 1977 there was a slim possibility I might play in a real NHL game. It happened quickly. Two days before, regular Buffalo goalie Gerry Desjardins suffered an eye injury in a game, an injury that caused his career to end early, as his vision never properly returned. The other goalie on Buffalo's roster was Al Smith, a journeyman who had played for Imlach in Toronto and bounced around the league for several seasons, almost always as a backup. Imlach also had two prime prospects stashed in the minors, both of whom he had drafted in June of 1976. The playoffs were approaching, and he had found out that morning about Desjardins's prognosis. Punch needed a first-line goalie if the Sabres were going to be able to make any kind of playoff run. The Cleveland Barons offered Imlach Gilles Meloche, who had always labored on losing teams but was respected in the league for his skills. Cleveland wanted a premier player for Meloche, for they knew Punch was over a barrel. There were a few more days before the trading deadline, so Punch had some wiggle room. He decided to really wiggle and take a chance on a rookie.

"I can get Meloche," he said late on the afternoon before the Sabres were to face the Minnesota North Stars at home. "But if one of our kids can really play, then I don't have to make the deal. We're gonna find out."

The rookie goalies were Don Edwards and Bob Sauve.

Edwards was playing for the Sabres' minor league affiliate in Hershey, Pennsylvania, while Sauve was on loan to Providence, Rhode Island, both American Hockey League teams. Punch phoned his pro scouts, who reported both rookies had a great shot at being a good big-leaguer. Satisfied it was worth the risk, he began making arrangements to summon one of them to Buffalo for the game the next night.

It turned out Sauve was playing that evening in the Canadian maritimes, so forget Sauve. Edwards, on the other hand, was with Hershey and a flight could bring him to the Sabres three hours before the scheduled faceoff against the North Stars. Imlach called owner Seymour Knox and explained what his plans were. He would look at Edwards, and if he was good enough, there would be no deal for Meloche.

I was in on all the conversations, alongside Punch in his office, and soon was in a little deeper. Imlach pulled a legal document from his desk drawer and passed it to me. "I should have done this years ago," he said. "This is an amateur tryout contract. Sign it, just in case we have to dress you sometime, like tomorrow night." I was stunned. Me? In goal? Dressing for an NHL game? I was 38 years old and not much of a goalie. "Listen," he said, "even if you dress, it's not likely you'll ever play. You're not afraid, are you?" I told him I was only afraid of making an ass of myself in front of 16,000 people who paid to see an NHL game, including NHL goaltending.

"No matter what, you're the only goalie for the morning skate tomorrow. I can't take the chance that Smitty gets hurt and Edwards doesn't get here on time. Then I'd have no goalies at all."

I wasn't upset he didn't care about the possibility I might get hurt that next morning. I was proud to be called on. I was thrilled that I had signed a contract, though I admit I complained about the money.

"Hell, you're not even worth that much," Imlach had replied, with a broad smile. "Take it or leave it." I still complained just for show, but he wouldn't come up even a dollar or two. I was too much in shock to continue what was a surreal conversation. I didn't even believe it myself. Me, the possible backup goalie in an NHL game. I couldn't eat and I hardly slept that night.

The next morning's pregame workout was only 35 minutes long, but I stayed on the ice much longer, taking shots from anyone who wanted extra practice. After I stripped and showered, I found my equipment had been carefully placed to dry quickly, and a game jersey and stocking were in my stall. I deliberately didn't look at the number. I didn't want to get my hopes up, yet I was secretly praying Edwards wouldn't make it in time. The day passed quickly as I was busy making preparations for my press box responsibilities, plus working alongside Rick Jeanneret on the radio broadcast. At 4:30 PM I dialed the dressing room and Christie answered. "He just walked in," Frankie told me. Edwards was there, and I felt better with that weight lifted off my shoulders, but worse because my idyllic dream wouldn't become reality. Just to sit on the bench and soak it all in during a game...to hear my name being announced on the public-address system...to skate out and back and know that thousands of fans were scratching their heads wondering why I was there instead of a pro.... Even today, those memories of possibility are part of me.

I climbed up to the press box about 6:00 PM for the 7:30 game and was busy with my duties until moving into the radio booth with Jeanneret at 7:15. My chief assistant, Leslie Brinkworth, was the only one upstairs who knew what my day had been about. I told her earlier that, yes, I might have to dress for the game and she would be taking over everything. She at first assumed I was joking. In fact, it took a few minutes to convince her I wasn't. But I had said to keep it quiet. If it happened, the world would know soon enough. The national anthems were scheduled for 7:27 and went off on time. Players from both teams lined up on the blue lines and restlessly stood for their conclusion.

The music ended, but before anyone even had a chance to sit, Al Smith skated a few feet toward the glass in front of the Knox brothers' seats and saluted them briskly, then skated off the ice toward the dressing room. I wondered why. Had Smitty decided to sit in the room in a fit of pique after not being selected to start? Probably, i thought, chiming in with pregame chatter as Jeanneret set up the opening faceoff. The puck hadn't yet dropped when a hand shook my shoulder. I turned and saw Leslie motioning to me.

"Mr. Imlach wants to talk to you right now," she said. I pushed the cough button that cut out my microphone and replied: "Tell him I'm on the air."

"Paul," she said, "it's an emergency. You've got to talk to him." I ran to the phone at the far end of the press box and Punch snarled these words. "Get down here and get dressed…right now." He hung up.

I was being called to my destiny, I thought, as I ran down the 103 stairs to the Aud floor level. I thought: "Whatever is going on, I am going on that ice. Smitty must be sick, or something crazy like that." I ran into the dressing room and stopped before Smith's empty stall. His goalie equipment was strewn about. Rip Simonick, the equipment manager, told me to start getting dressed as fast as I could. "Smitty came in here, pulled off all his stuff, got dressed, and ran out the door," he said. "Punch wants you to get ready and you'll go to the bench during a stop in play."

I was all thumbs and then some as I began dressing. Years of habit helped, as I followed my equipment routine quickly in spite of my stress. I had reached the moment when I was cinching the straps on my left goal pad when the bottom fell out. Or perhaps sanity returned to my life. NHL officials supervisor Frank Udvari, a onetime referee and a friend, walked into the room. "Paul, I'm sorry. You can forget about going out there tonight. You're not eligible. You weren't in the lineup the coach had to turn in ahead of time. There's nothing I can do."

I sat there unbelieving. But then I realized he was right. Deep inside, a little sigh escaped my soul, for I was so close to something I could not ever have dreamed up in the wildest conjectures as a boy listening to Foster Hewitt from Maple Leaf Gardens on a Saturday night. But close only counts in horseshoes, so I knew I had work to do. I stripped off my equipment, dressed, and headed up to the press box, sadder but wiser. What would have happened if I entered the game and blew easy shots because of being nervous? Would I lose whatever skills I had shaking in my skate boots before 16,000 people? What the hell was I thinking anyway? I was a 38-year-old overweight PR man, not a goalie—not in this league.

By the time I reached the press box I was calming down. Leslie asked me what happened, and I said I would explain later. Jeanneret asked me during a commercial break, but I sloughed it off. I knew that my close call was just that and didn't merit any special attention. So I kept it to myself for a long time, telling only my wife and a few close friends. The players knew, though, and several offered their sympathies, also reminding me it was a good thing I hadn't played. "You would have stunk," was one opinion, delivered to bust my chops. He was correct, I am pretty sure. But on dark, quiet nights when I review my life and the fun I had, I still wonder if that one night might have been a magic one for me. I'll never know, and thus I can play it out in my brain anytime I want to. In this daydream, I'm a star.

Al Smith not only walked out that night; he never returned to the Sabres. The team mailed him his last paycheck a few days later. Edwards became a league All-Star. And incidentally, he was the first star that night against the North Stars, stoning Minnesota in the 6–2 win.

I played goal off and on in practice for several more years but was retired by Scotty Bowman when he came to Buffalo. A bad knee had me gimping for years, and I retired at the same time from senior hockey.

Mr. Smith Comes to Buffalo

Derek Smith was called up to the Sabres at the same time as Don Edwards. Smith looked back in a recent interview: "I spent most of my first three years in Hershey [Pennsylvania]. It was a great town and I loved it. I was on a two-year contract but I was having so much fun, I was hoping they wouldn't call me up, which was kind of silly at the time. But I did get called up at the end of the third year and stayed up from that time on and realized that Buffalo was the place to be. In my second year, I got called up for one playoff game. In my third year, I was called up for half a dozen to a dozen games. In year four, I was up for good.

"I can't remember what line I was on. I do remember the fourth year, I did get a stint to play with Gilbert [Perreault] for a while. That was the year I think that both Punch and Marcel [Pronovost] were fired. And Billy Inglis came in as interim coach. I did play about 15 games on a line with Gilbert. I ended up getting 12 goals that year and most of them came from him.

"Gilbert was the heart and soul of the franchise. Absolutely. I grew up in London, Ontario, as a Montreal Canadiens fan because my dad was a Quebecer and Jean Beliveau came after that. Beliveau was always my idol growing up as a kid. I went to a junior game in London once and remember sitting way up at the top. The Junior Canadiens were in town and I watched this kid for the Junior Canadiens who I never heard of. It was Gilbert Perreault. I watched him play that game that night, and from that point on he became my idol. I was playing midget hockey at the time. Of course, down the road, we played on the same team and I was on the same line.

"He was just special. To watch him play was exactly the way I like to play, but he did things that no one else could do. And even to this day, he was my favorite player to watch. The moves he made; he just seemed to beam himself from one place to another. His lateral movement; no one else could do and no one has ever done. It was just magical to watch. You saw him and you knew every time he had the puck, something was going to happen. It would have been great to be a goalie then. You'd just wait at the net and wave at it. How many times did you see him score like that, leaving the goalie just waving in frustration.

"My game was as a playmaker. In junior, I was a goal scorer and a playmaker. The worst thing for me was fighting. I didn't have any part of that game. You didn't mind getting hit. You didn't mind going hard in the corners and hitting people. That wasn't my game. My game was, I could handle the puck and get it to the wingers. In those days, my line mates were Danny Gare and Tony McKegney. You didn't have to; they were looking for it all the time, whether they were in position or not. They were asking for it. My job was to get it to them, and that was the part of the game I liked. I liked setting up a play as much as scoring a goal. But as far as the fighting and the intimidation, that wasn't part of my game. I didn't like that part of it. I think I was in maybe nine fights as a pro in the American League and the National League. To show what a fighter I was, I only got two majors out of nine fights. How bad is that!"

Sauve Checks In

That same 1975 draft that brought Taro and Derek Smith also snared the tandem of goaltenders who would later win the Vezina Trophy, Don Edwards and a French-Canadian named Bob Sauve.

At 5'8", Sauve was close to Roger Crozier's size, though his style in goal was different. He played the classic standup way, cutting down angles and staying on his feet as much as possible.

"I was on loan the first year," recalled Sauve. "I went to Hershey a bit and I went to Charlotte in North Carolina. By the time I was sent down, there was no room in Hershey. Donnie Edwards was sent there before me, and Hershey had a Pittsburgh goal prospect on the roster. The Sabres were sharing the farm club with the Penguins.

"I ended up in the East Coast League, and we won the championship over there, which was nice. The next year I played in Charlotte for a while, and then I came up to Buffalo. I was up and down between Providence, then Hershey, until I finally stuck in Buffalo. At first I had to learn a little bit of English, but by the time I got to Buffalo, I think I was speaking the language all right. When I was in Montreal as a kid, and I played most of my minor league hockey with English people when I was in Laval. I was a junior for a while, so it didn't take too long [to learn the language]. It came back quick. The surrounding over there in Laval was real good because we had good people, a lot of good English people. And there were a lot of French there, too, so I lived with a little bit of everything.

"I was just a kid when I came to Buffalo, so playing in the NHL was a little overwhelming at first. I was with all the big boys.

Bob Sauve shared a Vezina Trophy in Buffalo.

I was raised in Montreal and followed the Canadiens' success in the '70s, so it was impressive to play against them. The Canadiens were my home team. At that point, they had such a machine, it was just unbelievable.

"We were very competitive against them. The Canadiens, they didn't like to play against the Sabres because we were successful against them. That's something I really remember. Then there were all those small dynasties, to play against Edmonton and Gretzky, and after that, the Islanders with Bossy. You don't see those dynasties in the NHL today."

Sauve said his time in hockey was different from today's NHL experience: "We just had more fun. It was looser then. But it was tougher to get your job. It was tougher for a young guy like me, or anybody else. I thought it was great because the veterans tried to protect themselves from the younger players coming in. Once you got in, you got the same thing. Which I think is great. You got the same protection, which was good. But I do think guys were just more loose. It was certainly fun. I remember we used to go, in Buffalo, for lunch after practice, not like once a week or so but almost after every practice. You'd think it would be 45 minutes or an hour, but Bert [Perreault] would grab the mike and sing and we'd be there for a while.

"Players today make more money but have less fun than we did. Life is more competitive today; and people's parties during the holidays would last for three days. Now the party-goers have to go back home because they are working the next day or are trying to be careful. I'm not saying it's wrong. We had more time. Remember, we'd leave on Friday night for a Saturday night game. The girls would get together at one house with the babies. You don't see that too often anymore. There was a lot more togetherness. I remember going out for dinner after games with all the players with their wives."

Sauve recalled the players and the teams that he hated to face: "I disliked playing against Mario [Lemieux]. He had a right-hand shot and long arms, and for me he was the toughest guy to stop. I couldn't stop him. Most of the time he was shooting from off wing on the power play. I really had a tough time playing against him for some reason. I had a really good time playing against Gretzky for some reason that I don't know. I guess Gretzky was probably better at that time all-around. You wanted to beat the best. For some reason we did better against him. But Mario was so tough it was unbelievable.

"I never had much success against Minnesota for some reason. So, it was one of those things. I couldn't play well against them. I couldn't play well in Buffalo or in Minnesota. That wasn't a great combination. Then again, you have to remember that then it wasn't like it is now. There were some expansion teams you could beat by putting your arms out wide. Expansion teams like Colorado; you could win by 10 goals, which you don't see today."

Now a successful player agent who deals with aggressive media in the Montreal area on a regular basis, Sauve had some observations about reporters in his playing days: "The press traveled with us. You could sit down and have a couple of beers with them. They were guys like Dick Johnston [hockey writer for the *Buffalo Evening News*]. You could tell him stuff and he knew what he could write and not write. We had this confidence in him. It was completely different from what it is today. Now it's more everybody for themselves. Everybody's trying to get a little bit ahead. I can't blame today's media. There are so many more involved. They all need to write something. It didn't seem to be that way in our day.

"They need to report, to get good stories, but they didn't need to create and report all the crap that is going on today. I think the players were a little more open about talking when I played. There were some boundaries. Now it's tough. It's a different ballgame. The media don't know the players; they're from all over the world. And now they get so much attention, you might trust three guys in the pack, but today there are 20 of them all looking for a different angle. There's something in there that's lost. The guys [players] are always being surrounded by people who look for them to make a slip."

Chapter 12
Hired to Be Fired

"You had the Cold War going on [with] the Communists, and a lot of the guys were Canadians, so we set out to show the Russians that we could skate with them and that we could outscore them, and we did."

−Rico Martin

The Coaching Merry-Go-Round

In the advertising business, there's a saying that the day you sign on a new account is just one day closer to the day you lose it. Coaching is a parallel experience. The day you get the job is merely the first day of the short period you'll have the job. At least that's the way it goes in North America's principal pro sports leagues, the NFL, the NBA, Major League Baseball, and the NHL.

One can be a career coach, though seldom in the same job. Pro sports coaches get used to buying and selling houses and the arrival and departure of moving vans. There is no job security. The money is great, but the competitive nature of the business means most coaches throw away too many hours a day reviewing video-tapes, "breaking them down," in case some observed tic in an opponent's players or playing style might be used to an advantage. No one has ever been able to satisfactorily explain why working 20 hours each day, seven days a week, analyzing a game being played by huge men in funny clothing and gargantuan equipment, is a noble objective, or even more effective. Everybody does it, so where's the edge?

Pro sports coaches are very different from us. Their lives revolve solely around wins and losses by men and women they can't really control, just hope to influence in ways that will lead to success in the games they play. The best coaches, it is said, are able to teach their players in the mysteries of their sport, making them able to perform better. But the dynamic of team sports results in coaching being only an educated guess.

How many times have we seen a team perform at a high level of excellence and defeat a highly rated opponent, then fall down and roll over against the opponent with a losing record? Is the coaching "good" the first time and "bad" the second? The inter-play of all the team's members much more determines a game's result than anything a coach could possibly say or do.

That's why coaches often have their own mantras. They need some kind of value system in their sport to justify their very exis-tence, not merely as a coach but also as a person. Coaches are tied to winning and losing much more than their players. Coaches come and go often and routinely. Rosters only change incrementally. The way the players perform determines whether coaches keep their jobs. But players are inconsistent, and by the professional level, some say, they can't be coached. This leaves us with coaches that are insecure, ego-driven, cocky but unsure, for they fail more than they ever succeed.

In a quarter century at the Sabres a long line of men moved through the coaching ranks as head coaches and assistants. It was often frustrating when they tried to get their theories and their directions through to a group of athletes who relied on their own skills and instincts rather than anything a coach told them.

Some NHL coaches try to change the complexion of a team by forcing a style of play and a set of on- and off-ice disciplines on players who aren't a fit for that style. Bad coaches tie ropes around their talent in an effort to establish who is boss or to follow their own muse, instead of evaluating a team's talent intelligently. Sometimes bad coaches drive their players a little crazy. Sometimes bad coaches are a little crazy themselves.

Successful coaches go with the flow. If talent (or lack thereof) demands a style that's defensive and careful, then a successful coach guides his team that way. If he's fortunate enough to have the skill players on offense, then he allows them to play that kind of game.

Punch Imlach was fortunate, as was Scotty Bowman later. They both were general managers as well as coaches in Buffalo. Both had the power to build the kind of team they would like to coach. It was a longer process for Imlach, who was given the culls of the rest of the league as his pro roster when the expansion Sabres entered the NHL in 1970. That list of players nobody else wanted was augmented by the number one pick in the summer's amateur draft.

Punch was the ultimate superstitious coach. He was bald as one can get without shaving one's head and constantly wore expensive beaver fedoras, behind the bench and just about everyplace else. Running a practice on skates, he would wear a Sabres baseball cap. The beaver fedoras were his more formal trademark and good-luck charms, at least when the Sabres won. When that happened he would wear the same hat for the next game, and the next, if the team kept winning or played to a tie. Losing hats were consigned to the scrap heap.

Bowman was less obvious with his superstitions but more obvious with his impatience. One day during practice in Memorial Auditorium, Scotty had been on the ice for just a minute or two when he determined that the ice surface was far below his standards. Bad ice can be a problem in many arenas, particularly the morning after a night game, when the crowd heats up a building and there's a lot of humidity. Scotty skated for a short time, then ordered one of the training staff to call the office of the Aud director and summon him to rink side.

The Aud director, Joe Figliola, was a political appointee by the City of Buffalo, which owned and operated the building. He had no building management background. He was a connected lawyer who later became a City Court judge. He was short, stocky, and usually mild-mannered and reasonable. This day, he had to be quick to avoid Bowman's ire. Scotty stormed off the ice when he saw Figliola standing behind the rink at the entrance from the Sabres dressing room. He began shouting at Figliola, complaining about how bad the ice was, how the city never made good ice, and so on. Figliola began retreating from Bowman, who towered over him on skates and was using his hockey stick as a pointer. The pointer kept getting closer to the Aud director's face.

Joe turned on his heel and started to walk away from Bowman, with a last remark aimed at retaining as much dignity as he could muster. Figliola left the rubber carpet used to keep players' skates from being dulled as they came off the ice. So did Bowman, still on skates. He began to run after Figliola, scraping his skate blades on the concrete and flapping his stick in the air as he continued to criticize the ice, the city, and Figliola. It was a sight: Figliola's stubby legs churning and Bowman's skates and legs akimbo as he tried to run on the thin blades over the concrete floor. After about a 50-foot sprint, Bowman gave up and returned to the dressing room, where a trainer repaired his nicked-up skate blades.

Imlach was volatile, but he had what could be called a romantic streak. If anyone showed loyalty to him, the team, the franchise, and so on, Imlach returned it in kind. There were many others who held coaching jobs with the Sabres in the first 25 years. But there were few assistants. Most teams in the '70s were coached by but one man, and often that man doubled as the GM. Imlach never had an assistant coach, nor did almost any of his counterparts.

The game is different today, with a head coach and usually at least two others behind the bench, one in charge of forwards and the other in charge of the defense. Following the first NHL expansion in 1967, and as a traditional part of the game, line and defense changes usually happened after one and a half to two minutes of play. It wasn't unusual to see the same power play unit and the same penalty killers on the ice for the duration of a minor (two-minute) penalty. That's because there were more whistles in the old NHL, and players stalled around more before the next faceoff. Today, stalling gets you a penalty. In 1970, it got you extra rest.

Now the game is played on the fly, with line changes and defensive changes happening in 45 seconds to a minute. It's easy to understand why there's one coach for the defensive line and another for the forwards. Throw in goalie coaches (everyone has one today, at least a part-timer) and there are 120 men making a living as coaches in the NHL. The year before expansion, there were six coaches and a total of 90 skaters that would dress for games, plus six goalies (no backup goalies were allowed in uniform). NHL coaching jobs fell almost exclusively to ex-NHL players. There were many exceptions, of course. Imlach and Bowman never played in the NHL. But there were no coaches out of the college ranks and none from overseas. Everyone had a pro hockey pedigree. If there was ever a good ol' boy network, it was coaching in the NHL.

Some assistants came in the door and out again so quickly that we didn't really get to know them at all. Red Berenson was a Buffalo assistant under Scotty who went on to coach NCAA championship teams at the University of Michigan. Red was one of the quiet ones, often found up front in his office, puffing on his pipe and making notes.

Another coaching quiet man was Allan Stanley, who was enshrined in the Hockey Hall of Fame in 1981. Stanley spent his career mostly in Toronto and was brought in to work with Buffalo's defense. It wasn't that Stanley didn't communicate with players. He just didn't have much to say to anyone. "Silent Sam" was his nickname.

Jim Roberts was his polar opposite. As an NHL winger with St. Louis and later with Scotty Bowman in Montreal, Roberts was what coaches call a "grinder." He wasn't a good skater, wasn't a good scorer, and wasn't a goon. But he always held up his end in any fight and played a rugged defensive game. Jim was matched with the opponent's best winger, who he would try to obliterate into the ice or into the boards. Dogged as a player, Roberts was the kind of teammate who stood up in any situation and gave it his best. His heart was his best skill, and it gave him a solid big-league career.

Jimmy was loud, profane, and constantly chomping a cigar in his years as a coach in Buffalo. He was as much a cheerleader as an analytical coach, the same guy in his new job as he had been in uniform. The mercurial Bowman needed someone who could get through to his players on the personal side of things. "You know Scotty," Roberts would say to a player who came to him with a complaint about the way Bowman was treating him. Roberts was intensely loyal to Bowman, but he also served as the "good cop" when Scotty played the bad one. Roberts was a free spirit, more likely to ride a tractor down a country road singing at the top of his lungs than he was to dine formally. And he truly loved cigars.

Joe the Crow

Joe Crozier's time as Buffalo's coach was the stuff of which a mystery story is made. Joe had been a coach with Imlach when both had financial interests in minor league franchises. Crozier was a journeyman minor league defenseman who became friends with Punch

Joe Crozier coached the Sabres first playoff team.

along the way, and their friendship turned into profit with teams in Vancouver and Rochester. Joe the Crow loved his nickname, using crow drawings on custom greeting cards and treasuring a stuffed crow someone had given him. He had been coaching in Rochester in the 1971–72 season when Imlach suffered a major heart attack and was sidelined for much of the season. Punch had already set Crozier as his replacement should anything happen to him, so it was just an hour's ride for Crozier to his interim coaching job. Crozier couldn't guide the Sabres into the playoffs that season, but he was given the job by his mentor, and the next season he took the team to its first postseason competition.

Once described in print by the old Winston Churchill line about "a mystery wrapped in an enigma," Crozier was just that to his players and everyone else who worked with him. He brought a Roman Catholic priest into the dressing room, and the padre soon was telling everyone that he was the Sabres' team chaplain. Joe encouraged his players to discuss their personal problems with the priest. The problem was that there wasn't supposed to be a team chaplain.

There was a split in the dressing room when it came to Crozier. A few players thought he was impossible to play for. Most of the others were amused by his strange ways and found him a good coach. He was highly critical of mistakes by some players and berated them in front of their teammates. Yet others whom he liked got a free pass from public criticism.

It was Crozier's style to be divisive. He seemed to thrive on creating tensions where none had existed before. By the 1973–74 season, it was becoming obvious to the media and many of the Sabres staff that Crozier wanted to succeed his old friend Imlach as general manager. And he wanted it to happen then, not some day in the fuzzy future. Crozier ran a guerrilla campaign for the job, constantly leaking stories to one newspaper reporter, stories about possible trades and player movements that really belonged to the GM's position. Imlach became angry, and when Crozier stopped talking to him, Punch realized the situation was reaching critical mass.

"I'll be damned if I don't have to use the trainers as spies to find out what's going on down there," he complained to me.

It was suggested he have it out with Crozier, but Punch wouldn't do that. They had been friends for decades, and Punch was reluctant to put Crozier on the carpet. He knew that Crozier and his supporters were campaigning with the Knox brothers and other team stockholders for Imlach's "retirement for health reasons." Punch wouldn't bend, nor would he criticize his coach publicly or privately.

"He's my friend," Punch told me. "No matter how much he is ticking me off right now, he's my friend. And don't you forget it."

Crozier's coaching habits sometimes were bizarre. He would take a wooden chair to the center ice faceoff dot when he was angry with his team, sit there and sip coffee, and watch them go through the most boring skating drill in hockey. That drill works like this: all players skate in the same direction around the perimeter of the ice and sprint between the blue lines on the straight sections of the oval. The drill is used mostly to stretch legs at the start of a practice, but 90 minutes of blue line sprints is enough to drive a player to drink. The only drinking at those practices was done by Crozier, who would knock off three or four cups of coffee watching his bored charges.

Joe often used a punishment practice like this after a bad performance. Many players understood the punishment idea but complained they were just wasting time instead of improving team skills. Whatever magic Crozier had exhibited in coaching Buffalo to a playoff spot the year before had disappeared in his second season, and Crozier was gone to the World Hockey Association by the next fall.

When Scotty Bowman held the GM's job alone, without coaching duties intruding, he became ill at ease with his coaches. He had hired them, but he seemed uncomfortable with them. Scotty, after all, had only been a coach in the NHL until he was hired in Buffalo. He found that doing both jobs, GM and coach, required separate skill sets, and of necessity he had to leave coaching if he wanted to be GM. He couldn't very well fire himself as GM and stay on as a coach. But Scotty wasn't the most successful coach in league history by accident. He knew how to do that job as well as anyone, and when as GM he felt that his coach wasn't up to snuff, Scotty turned to himself as a remedy to the problem.

Those on the inside of the Sabres office could tell when one of Scotty's coaches was soon to lose his job. Bowman would stop talking to the guy. He would walk right by the open door of the coach's office and totally ignore him. It was nerve-wracking for the coach to watch himself become a nonperson in Scotty's view. Jimmy Roberts, for one, refused to accept the fact that his old coach in Montreal would treat him that way as a prelude to getting fired. Roger Neilson was more pragmatic. He had been fired before and would be fired again, so he was used to being left to dangle by a general manager.

Although the coaching carousel in Buffalo revolved a number of times during the team's first quarter century, not one of those coaches was a goaltending specialist. Things have changed radically since then. Today every team, including Buffalo, has a full- or part-time goaltending coach. In the '70s and '80s, teams carried two goalies who dressed for every game, though in most cases, one would get substantially more starts than the other. Coaches knew when their goaltenders were good, but they usually didn't know why. They just looked up at the scoreboard for validation.

Montreal's outstanding and eccentric goalie Jacques Plante wrote a book on the position in the early '60s and even some big-league goalies gobbled it up for advice. In the times of the "Original Six", teams only carried one goalie, who was expected to play every game. These goalies came from across Canada and usually ended up in the position as a kid because they were too small to be a forward or a defenseman, or didn't skate well enough. These goalies had been their own coaches throughout their careers, unless they were lucky enough to have a youth coach who had played the position. Goalies generally arrived in the NHL as totally self-made players. Their only instruction came from a coach who would yell at them to stand up in the net, now and always.

That isn't bad advice, but today's NHL goalies hardly ever stand up to stop a puck, so that style of play is long gone. The game was different through the first two decades of expansion, and goalies suffered through the banana-blade stick and rocket-like slap shots by figuring it out for themselves. It was a miracle that no NHL goalie was killed by a shot after the curved stick came into play in the 1960s and made the slap shot a potential killer. Except for Plante, who had adopted a mask after nearly losing half his face to a shot during a game, there were few goalies before expansion who wore masks in a game. Their faces usually looked like day-old chewing gum with stitch furrows, but goalies just didn't wear masks. It wasn't a macho thing. They genuinely believed a mask interfered with their ability to see and stop the puck. With only six big-league goalie jobs available, no one was willing to cut down on vision to save himself from injuries. Wearing a mask might mean you'd lose your job.

Buffalo had a goalie in the first season who didn't wear a mask except in practice. Joe Daley had kicked around the league and the high minors and always played with his bare face hanging out. I asked him once why he didn't don a mask in games.

"Practice is much more dangerous than games," he told me. "You take hundreds of shots sometimes in practice, and everybody is firing away without being checked. That's when a mask is smart. In a game, maybe you get 30 or 35 shots, and you can usually see them all. If I can see it, I wouldn't get hit in the face." It must be noted, however, that Joe adopted a face mask for games in the next season, his last with the Sabres.

Buffalo had no goalie coach when two young Sabres goaltenders drafted in 1975 ended up with the team at the same time. Bob Sauve and Don Edwards teamed up to win the Vezina Trophy for Buffalo in 1980, the award then given to the team that allowed the fewest goals during the schedule. They fed off each other, constantly analyzing each other's style and talking about shooters and ways to play them. Edwards was a bob-and-weave goaltender who was up and down much more than Sauve, who consciously or unconsciously played a style like Jacques Plante, standing up and playing the angles. Things had changed since Buffalo had come into the league in 1970, just 10 years earlier. Sauve had never played goal at any level without a mask and was incredulous one day at practice when I took dozens of slap shots without my mask. That prompted him to describe me as "crazy."

Since they didn't have a specialty coach, goalies were always asking someone else to look for their weaknesses. Some would study game video in an effort to identify why they were getting beat in certain situations. Dave Dryden once asked me to see if I could determine why he was leaking on medium- and long-range shots. I looked at his setup in several practices and told him he was sitting back on his skates too much, making it hard for his 6'2" body to move laterally. I said he should shift his weight forward. I honestly have no clue whether that was the problem, but Dryden took my comments to heart and applied them. Goaltending is half confidence, and when a goalie thinks he has identified a problem in his style, he gains confidence and usually plays better. Dryden improved markedly against those shots that bothered him before. I couldn't ever pretend to be a goaltending coach, but that's how desperate goalies were for outside counsel when teams didn't have anyone to work with them.

The expansion NHL did add one kind of new coach in the late 1960s and early '70s. The "strength" or "conditioning" coach was usually a part-timer from a local gym or health club who would come in after on-ice practice and run the players through aerobic, strength, and flexibility exercises. Teams began loading up weight and workout rooms with sophisticated and expensive equipment. Now that kind of approach is routine, even in golf. But it was a big change from the pre-expansion NHL.

Big-league hockey players were a different breed before the league doubled its size in 1967. The average player had a summer job. Playoffs were over by mid-April, as only four teams fought their way through two series to win the Stanley Cup. Salaries were disgraceful, considering that the NHL was the premier league in the sport. Players needed those off-season jobs shilling for breweries and the like to make a decent living.

When training camp opened in September players used the two- to three-week period to get in shape, lose a few pounds, and sharpen their hockey skills with a few desultory exhibition-game performances in small-town rinks across Ontario and Quebec. Strength and conditioning were a very personal matter, and some players got by on talent alone, as the game wasn't as fast and aerobically demanding as it is today. There weren't many hockey rinks around in the off-season that were making ice, so NHL players might not skate for months between seasons.

Since the situation was the same for all NHL players, no one was far ahead or far behind the others when a season opened. Coaching then was more like generalship than being a first lieutenant in charge of an infantry company. An NHL coach involved in tactics every game—like a lieutenant—but was looking at the long haul—like a general. There was less coaching on individual skills. Talent and personal skills development got a player to the NHL. He wasn't going to receive much skills coaching after he reached the big leagues. It was more game tactics and team style. A player would have to work on his individual skills by himself.

The Russians Were Coming

The Cold War was on in 1976, and the ice hockey version was between the pros from North America and the teams of the Soviet Union's elite league. The Soviet Central Red Army was reputed to be the best club team in the Russian league, and the second best was the Wings of the Soviet. That team was sponsored by the state-owned and operated aviation industry. The Russians scheduled an eight-game North American tour to play against NHL teams in NHL arenas, with half the games to be played by the Central Red Army team and half by the Wings. Each club's lineup was augmented with five players from other elite league teams.

Buffalo was scheduled to play the Wings in Memorial Auditorium just after the New Year, with the chance to scout the Russians when they played the Pittsburgh Penguins six nights earlier. The Sabres were driven to a peak they seldom had achieved by Imlach, who took the game as a personal challenge—the Free

World against the Communist World. He could barely contain himself when it came to talking about the Soviet political system. But he was an admirer of their hockey system, where speed and precision, head-manning the puck, and crisscrossing forwards as they entered the offensive zone were at the heart of the Russian style of play.

The Russians taught the world much about hockey, with their game usually on the longer and wider international ice surface. Their teams were free skating, didn't body check much (unlike NHL clubs), and relied on precision passing and positional play. Imlach had built a Buffalo team that used speed, but also had a big, powerful defense in Schoenfeld, Hajt, Jerry Korab, Lee Fogolin, and Jocelyn Guevremont.

Imlach received a videotape of the Wings' win over Pittsburgh on Friday January 2. He called in his coach, Floyd Smith, and scouting director, John Andersen, who had taken in the Russian win in Pittsburgh. Punch ran the tape forward and backward, sitting in an improvised video room next to Seymour Knox's Auditorium office.

"There has to be a way to exploit their style," he told Andersen and Smith. "Watch Pittsburgh get sucked into playing right with them, when the Russians crisscross, the back-checkers are going with them, and either getting picked off or just plain out of position."

For hours that day and into the evening, Imlach reviewed the game tape. His answer to the Soviet Wings? "We have to stay in our lanes, play a kind of zone defense in the neutral zone, and hit them every chance we get," he said. "We can't be caught chasing them all around or we'll lose."

Imlach didn't have to do a thing to jack up his team emotionally. Rick Martin recalled: "I was as ready to play that game as I would ever be. I could hardly wait to get on the ice." When Buffalo came on the ice before a Cold War–sensitive sellout crowd, Martin exploded through the entrance gate. He wasn't the only one of the Sabres who could hardly wait.

Jerry Korab was the biggest Sabre of them all. A fierce (when angered) and powerful defenseman, Korab was 6'3", weighed 220 pounds, and had the indelicate nickname "King Kong," or simply "Kong" to his teammates. He had been traded to Buffalo from Vancouver nearly midway through the 1973-74 season, after two earlier years with the Blackhawks. With black hair and a black mustache that made him appear to be a giant Cossack, Korab was a physically imposing player who sometimes was diffident on the ice.

"At first as I was growing up to play hockey, I knew because of my size I would have to be aggressive and tough, but actually it didn't work out that way for me," Korab said. "I kind of just played. That was my style. I didn't go out of my way to fight anybody or to impress anybody. I was an aggressive player and I was also the type of player that you hear 'don't wake the friendly giant.' Most of the time I was not quiet, but if you left me alone, I wouldn't bother anybody.

"When I was traded I found out what the coaches would say when they came into Buffalo and were playing against me. Dave Lewis, of the Los Angeles Kings, was my good friend and he'd say: 'Well, Al Arbour used to say if anyone hits him, they're fined $500. Don't wake him up! If you're going to hit somebody, hit somebody else. We don't need him running around the ice after us.' If we lost I got more frustrated and aggravated than most. I got upset and more aggressive. I don't think there's anybody who likes losing or making a mistake and causing a goal."

When Korab hit the ice against the Wings of the Soviet he also started banging anything in a Russian jersey. Every shift, from the game's beginning, Korab took a bead on the Russian winger coming up his board side, or anyone who dared get near the Buffalo goal crease occupied by goalie Gerry Desjardins. And he didn't miss, delivering lusty body checks that at times had the Buffalo crowd on its feet.

"I thought that was phenomenal really, an opportunity to play against the Russians," Korab recalled. "I guess emotionally and physically I gave it everything I was. I was really hyped with that game, and actually Punch came in before the game and he said, 'If there ever was a game I want to win, this is the one I want to win." He really got everyone pumped up. I think maybe I played well, but if I played well it was because we all played well together and maybe I just stood out a little more that night. I just thought everybody played awesome. I wish I could get the tape of that game, believe me."

(Editor's note: I was able to find a tape of that game, which he sent to Korab, who made copies for his friends and family as a Christmas present.)

The Sabres attacked the Wings like antiaircraft flack, scoring twice in the game's first seven minutes to put the heat on immediately. Korab assisted on the second goal by Gilbert Perreault.

"I was fortunate to play on probably the three greatest lines in hockey, but if I had to choose one, I would probably go with the French Connection," said Korab. "One reason was the way they played together. A lot of finesse, quick.... They could all skate, they could all shoot, and they were all goal scorers. They did everything so well when they played together. I think because each of them respected the others so much, that was the reason why they played so well. That's probably why I liked them the most, and I played with them longer than any of those other lines. They became not just players but great friends on and off the ice. I'd love to play with them again if I had a choice."

Rick Martin scored next, making it 3–0. The Russians got one back. Martin scored again 38 seconds later, though a late goal by the visitors made it 4–2 at the end of the first period. Martin has a real enmity to this day toward the Soviet hockey system. In 2007 he told the student newspaper at the University of Buffalo: "You had the Cold War going on [with] the communists, and a lot of the guys were Canadians, so we set out to show the Russians that we could skate with them and that we could outscore them, and we did."

In the second period, the Sabres scored five more times, driving Alexander Sidelnikov from the nets. Korab continued to apply the hammer, plus he scored a pretty goal on assists from Martin and Robert and assisted on a goal by Danny Gare.

The third period extended the rout. Gare scored again, with

A souvenir pennant from the blowout victory over the Soviets.

Freddie Stanfield and Brian Spencer also getting on the board. The Sabres outshot the Russians 46–22 for the game, and if Desjardins had been sharper, the final score might have been 12–2. The Sabres still blew the doors off the Wings in a final score of 12–6.

The Soviet Wings went on to win their next two games against NHL opponents, ending up with three out of four in North America. The Buffalo drubbing, however, was the biggest defeat ever suffered by the Russians in international club play. The next night, when the Sabres skated onto the Forum ice in Montreal to play the Canadiens, the team received an extended standing ovation.

Bill Hajt explained that he had a premonition that would happen after the game in Buffalo the night before. "I remember we went out for dinner after the game. I told my mom and dad at dinner that something special was going to happen tomorrow. The fans didn't let me down. They did exactly what I told my mom and dad they were going to do. We came out on the ice for the start of the game and the Montreal fans gave us a two-minute standing ovation. The adrenaline I had…the feeling I had…it was basically Canada against the Soviet Union that series. It was like all of Canada was standing up and cheering for us. How often do you ever see that? A standing ovation in the other team's arena? I remember we went out that night to beat the Canadiens 4–2. You don't forget those things."

Chapter 13
The Call
of the Game

*"In his hosting days, Ted Darling could
be conceived as the id to Don
Cherry's modern-day insufferable ego."*

–Paul Wieland

The Voice

The most important figure in early Sabres history wasn't the gifted center Gil Perreault or the Stanley Cup-winning coach, Punch Imlach.

The key man those days was a barber's son from Kingston, Ontario, who was a bad skater and never made a dime from his on-ice skills. But off the ice, Edgar Lee Darling was the best and the brightest part of the new Sabres front-office staff in Buffalo. Edgar Lee, son of Bill, was known all his life as Ted and is known even today as one of the best play-by-play broadcasters in the history of the NHL.

He was more than that, of course. He knew the game, and he understood how to pass along that knowledge without over-calling or resorting to the clichés and malapropisms used by nearly every other broadcaster in hockey then and more so today.

His baritone was never theatrical, but it was comfortable to the ear. Ted's voice complemented the action, never upstaged it; Ted understood that the viewers were tuning in to see the game, not listen to him, so he never called attention to himself. Ultimately, Ted's dignified, on-air demeanor was comforting and never sounded as if it were staged. His voice sometimes dropped an octave to add dramatic timber to his game call, but only when the moment was itself dramatic. It would creep up an octave, too, when he was making a series of lightning calls on shots and rebounds.

When you talked to Ted on a street corner, he sounded exactly as he sounded on the air. There was no artifice to his skill. He was the same person off the air as on the air, and since Buffalo has often been called the "city of no illusions," Ted fit in perfectly in the community, where the best broadcasters for generations have seemed to be real folks.

Darling was hired after a clever ploy on his part in an effort to get the job. The NHL was adding both Buffalo and Vancouver in the fall of 1970, and that meant two more big-league announc-ing jobs were up for grabs in the months running up to the opening faceoff. Ted had been the intermission host on the

Hockey Night in Canada telecasts in Montreal for several years.

The intermission host slot was a big-time job in Canadian sports TV before the advent of cable network coverage nationally. Then there was only one *Hockey Night*. And when you had a job on *Hockey Night in Canada*, you had reached a pinnacle in sports broadcasting in the country. It was a journalist's job, with interviews the main thrust and conversations with serious analytical guests thrown in. Today, intermission programming on Canada's network coverage of the sport sometimes gets more attention than the games themselves thanks to the clown prince of hockey, former minor league defenseman and current major league blowhard, Don Cherry. He and intermission host Ron MacLean spew silliness, venom, and controversy from coast to coast every Saturday night, and night after night during the Stanley Cup playoffs.

In his hosting days, Ted Darling could be conceived as the id to Cherry's modern-day insufferable ego. Enthusiastic but measured, knowledgeable but not a know-it-all, Ted spoke to English-speaking viewers of the Canadiens telecasts with skill and warmth.

Darling Gets the Job

It's not likely Darling would have ended up doing play-by-play in Montreal. The English-language job was held by Danny Gallivan, a French Canadian who was legendary to his listeners and viewers, and who—in fact—held the job for two decades after Ted left to join the new Sabres organization. Waiting in the wings for Gallivan to retire was the equally famous Dick Irvin, son of a famous Canadiens coach.

Darling knew expansion of the NHL was his best chance to make bigger bucks and a bigger name for himself, though the latter never seemed very important to him. After the amateur draft in Montreal in June, Buffalo at least had a paper roster, a list of names of players drafted from other NHL teams as part of the expansion fee and a bunch of rookies from junior hockey selected in the amateur portion of the draft process.

Ted made up a projected Buffalo lineup before any of them

had laced on a skate for the Sabres. He went into a sound booth in Montreal, where he did a mock play-by-play call of an imaginary Sabres game against the Canadiens. To his own voice, Ted added a background tape of crowd and ice effects from a game in the Montreal Forum. He arranged for an engineer to bring the noise up at the proper times, and working from a script of his own devices, he also managed to have the new Sabres beat the Canadiens in the play-by-play.

"The game that never was" ended up on a cassette tape. The tape ended up in the mail to the Sabres, where Imlach was able to hear Darling's rendition of his new team's imaginary win over Stanley Cup champion Montreal. It was a match made in hockey heaven, the best from among dozens of tapes that came in applying for the job. Darling was quickly invited for an interview. A job offer followed.

Ted was in his thirties when the Sabres beckoned, and he brought his wife, Sheila, and four children to the area, where they settled at first in suburban Amherst. The Darlings soon were as popular with neighbors as Ted was to become on the air. Ted and his brood were just folks. They didn't just pretend at friendship. They were the real thing, and Ted's infectious laugh, dark horn-rimmed glasses, and quirky sense of humor were a physical and emotional benchmark for the new Sabres office.

His mates there found Ted willing to do just about anything, take on any assignment cheerfully, and work all the hours needed to get the team off the starting mark. "I figured," he told me later, "that the only way I could keep this job was to make sure the Sabres were successful in the community as well as on the ice."

From the day Ted joined the new team at its Peterborough, Ontario, training camp, Darling was the public media image of the Sabres. Later he would be called the "Voice of the Sabres" in programs and yearbooks, and he preferred that title to any other.

The Voice had a face, a body, and that sense of humor, and Ted hauled them all throughout western New York and nearby Ontario hundreds of times that first couple of years. He appeared at Scout meetings, rubber chicken luncheons and dinners run by service clubs of every stripe, sports nights, school assemblies, bar and bat mitzvahs, and baptisms, and he once did the play-by-play of a table hockey game at a summer picnic. That engagement was the result of donating his play-by-play services to the local public television station as an auction item. It was a hell of a picnic. I was his color man, and we kept our announcing throats moist with many picnic beers.

Because Darling was genuine, sounded that way on the air, and appeared that way on TV, he quickly became a fan and community favorite. When approached by anyone, anytime, he was invariably friendly and would stop other things in his life to chat with an adult fan or a kid who just wanted to know what "Gil Perreault is really like."

The Puckish Gag

Darling was also a bit of a squirrel, and his sense of humor—even better, his sense of fun—dovetailed with mine to perfection. Thus was born a team made in the heaven that exists for those who pull silly jokes and stunts. One of Ted's best running gags had to do with the identity of the fan who caught a puck when one entered the stands during play. To this day there are still fans of the old Sabres who half believe his version of how he knew the puck catcher.

The Darling method worked this way. When a puck flew off the ice, and as soon as Ted could determine that it hadn't injured a fan, he would say, "That one's caught by a fan from West Seneca" or some other Buffalo suburb, if not the city itself. He often dropped in Canadian references to communities near the Fort Erie border crossing to Buffalo, and after a few weeks nearly every town, city, and village on both sides of the border had been cited by him during a broadcast call.

Television didn't disrupt the gag. If a camera showed a close-up of the puck catcher, only that puck catcher would know whether he or she was from the town Ted referred to on the air. Since the fan sat in the arena and was not watching the telecast, no one could correct Ted's "error" anyway.

As the years went along, Darling started to know the locations of so many fans' season-ticket seats in Buffalo's Memorial Auditorium (rarely did season tickets change hands) that he was occasionally able to identify a fan by name and town when he saw the puck go into the crowd.

However, the gag nearly backfired one night on a cable telecast. I was in the big production truck directing. When Ted identified a fan by name, I called in a tight shot of the fan who had caught the puck. The fan, however, was at the game with a lady friend, one not his wife. Ted knew the fan, and did he get a scalding phone call the next day. We never found out who was awarded custody of the puck: the wife or the girlfriend.

After several years of the running gag, Ted announced what he said was the real secret about his ability to identify puck catchers in the stands. On that night's telecast he explained that each seat in Memorial Auditorium was wired into the Sabres' new central computer system, meaning the Sabres could get an instant report on the seat owner for any seat in the house on a computer screen.

"I just type in the seat location on my computer here in the booth," Ted told viewers, "and I get the name back in a flash." Ted said he had a blown-up Aud seating chart on the wall to his left to make sure he made the right seat call into the computer. Darling also extended this unique skill to road games as the years went by. In Montreal, he would identify the puck catchers in the Forum by their neighborhood. "That one's grabbed by a fan from Westmount," he would tell fans back in western New York.

He was at his best as a play-by-play man because he worked essentially as a journalist, not as a shill for the team that employed him or as a hype artist who sounded as if his pants were much too tight. When you listened to Ted Darling, you knew his call on radio would reflect the game in front of him. If Ted became excited and his voice rose above its usual baritone foundation, you listened more closely. This was a moment to play close attention. Something was really happening on that ice in front of him.

Concentrating on a radio call of a hockey game is difficult at best, and those announcers who sound like every pass and shot is spectacular soon wear out the listener's ears. They are fundamentally dishonest.

When Ted moved from mostly radio in Buffalo (the Sabres started out in 1970–71 with only eight games on television—all from the road) to mostly television (in his later years there were only four to eight games on radio versus TV), his accurate and level call fit the visual medium perfectly.

Ted didn't have to hype what you saw before you, and in fact, hyping television calls of hockey games is so offensive it isn't even funny. Yet many announcers still do it, some because they're stuck with a simulcast with radio, a situation in which neither medium is satisfactory even in the hands of the best announcers.

We had a rule in those days about first names. Ted and I traveled with the Sabres players. We were employees of the club, friends of many of those first Buffalo players. However, on the air we never used their first names only. It was "Gil Perreault" or "Perreault," but never "Gil." Same deal with nicknames. Ted would use them rarely, and only in second reference. He might say, "Dominic Hasek—the Dominator," but never just "the Dominator makes the save." It was that attention to detail that made Ted's work among the best ever in the NHL.

The first broadcast of my career with Buffalo was alongside Ted in the fall of 1970. As a new on-air color man (the terms *commentator* and *analyst* weren't in vogue then), I was on edge and skittish walking into the radio booth to sit down next to Darling.

"Just remember two things," he told me. "The first is that this job isn't fun, even though it is. If you tell people the job is fun, the word will get back to the owners, and they'll think they are paying you too much.

"The second thing is to make sure you keep announcing the score when you're doing radio. Don't assume your listener knows the score. He may just have tuned in, or has been away from the radio for a few minutes. Give the score often."

Darling showed me a two-minute egg timer he kept in front

of him during every broadcast. "It's to remind me to mention the score at least that often," he said.

Ted did it that way for his entire career. Once television arrived with the ability to keep a constant scoreboard on screen, that need wasn't as vital, but he still announced the score regularly out of habit.

"You're nuts; you know that, don't you?" was Darling's first reaction to my escapades revolving around my favorite holiday, April Fools' Day. As the Sabres public relations man, I had the where-withal, the budget, and the tools to use media communication for the good of the company, and I usually did. I also used them for a good time, pulling off decades of gag press releases and worse on that day of the year. Sabres ownership and top management went along with them all, usually agreeing with Ted, but laughing nearly every time as I poked fun at the seriousness with which Americans take their relationships with professional sports teams.

By the time I turned my April Fools' attentions to television in the early 1980s I was already known for being, shall we politely say, "eccentric," and television broadcasts became my new playground for my quirky, sophomoric sense of humor. That was when Darling proved to me he belonged in the Hockey Hall of Fame, or at least next to me in the Hockey Hall of Infamy. He joined in every gag I wanted to try, thinking of many himself, and poked fun at himself with outlandish on-air costumes and behavior each April first.

One year he opened the broadcast wearing one of his wife Sheila's blond wigs. (This was during that thankfully brief period in North American culture when normally sane housewives bought wigs that they wore over their real hair, resulting in more Harpo Marx look-a-likes than one can believe.) Darling appeared to be a Harpo of his own making that night, calmly facing the studio camera and discussing the upcoming game against Quebec without even cracking a smile while viewers all over upstate New York stared at a grown man in a curly blond wig. That was the Ted I knew, and color man Mike Robitaille shared the opening with him on camera. He reached over to Darling, poked at the wig, and asked, "Ted, what did you do to your hair?" Ted never flinched and didn't even acknowledge the question, and another night of silliness was under way.

The real fun with Ted lay in the fact that fans just didn't expect him to act like a damned fool, so when he did, they were unsure how to react.

He knew the sport, was able to provide insight and critical analysis even as he followed the puck and the flow of the game, and added a sense of joy and excitement even to the most boring of games. Ted was lucky during his career. The NHL was a scorer's league then, with players such as Guy Lafleur, Phil Esposito, Marcel Dionne, Wayne Gretzky, and dozens of others, including Buffalo's French Connection line, who were able to bring crowds to their feet in arenas across the continent with their brilliant goal-getting skills.

Darling's story took a different and tragic turn, but first and foremost he should be remembered for his ability to give Buffalo a big-league image from the moment he stepped aboard during training camp in 1970. It was 24 years later when a failing Ted Darling was inducted into the Hockey Hall of Fame. His progressive four-year battle against Pick's disease was heartbreaking to his family, friends, and all the Sabres family.

Chapter 14
A Stanley Cup Dream Revisited

"I thought we had the better team as far as skills. It just happened that Bernie Parent came up large for them and we couldn't put it by him."

—Freddie Stanfield

The Sabres Stanley Cup Final team from 1974–75, coached by Floyd Smith.

Hits and Misses

The peak moment of the Perreault years in Buffalo came in May of 1975 when the Sabres faced the defending Stanley Cup champion Philadelphia Flyers in the final series. The Flyers were known as the Broad Street Bullies by the media, and the nickname was appropriate. Dave Schultz, Don Saleski, and Ed Van Impe were among the meanest, toughest players in the NHL, and their captain and center, Bobby Clarke, combined talent with a stick he used like a surgeon. Playing against the Flyers was no fun for anyone anytime, because there were few in Coach Fred Shero's lineup that didn't buy into the Flyers' style of nasty play. Back in goal, Bernie Parent was arguably the best money net-minder in the game. The Sabres had been the second-highest-scoring team in the regular season, but Parent shut them down nearly every game, with the Cup going to Philadelphia in six games.

Some of those who played for Buffalo in that series have bittersweet memories. Some still sound disappointed. Jerry Korab was luckier than most. He played in a Cup Final more than once.

"In my first five years in hockey, I was in the Stanley Cup Finals three times and never got back after that," Korab recalled. "When my friends ask, 'Did you ever win the Stanley Cup?' I say I was there three times and they say, 'That's fantastic.' But I say, 'I never got there; we never won.' That's really everyone's goal, to win the Stanley Cup. As it stands now, I'm never going to win one, and I know a lot of guys that have and that's what you want to do, and it's probably the one thing in my career that I'm sad about. I'm probably not the only one in the National Hockey League who didn't win a Stanley Cup. When you had all the opportunities that I had and you came out on the other end, it's not a good feeling and you still think about it. As time goes by, you still think about those opportunities you had to win it. It still bothers me."

But Korab cherishes his life in hockey. "I'd do it all over again. No question. I'd do it the same way. I didn't come up the easy way, but I had a great life, a great career. I met a ton of fans and they still remain my friends, so it was something special, and that's my life and it still is. A lot of my friends are in coaching, general managers, things like that. It's amazing that from the years that we played that we still keep in contact with each other and families and their sons and daughters when they get married. That was a special time. People are amazed when they see us get together.

"When I got inducted into the Sabres' Hall of Fame, a lot of my friends from Chicago came down. I had a big party at the Hilton Hotel afterwards. Gilbert [Perreault] was there, Rene [Robert], and most of the guys from the team. They came there and it was like people never left. It was like you were here and were just having another party, and you've been gone for such a long time and you come back and it's like you never left. You can't put your finger on it, but the camaraderie is still there after all these years. Even when I left and Schony left and then other guys left, the thing was we still were close. I don't think there was anyone from that team that I hadn't talked to or known what they're doing or know what's happening with their family. It's amazing."

Freddie Stanfield had come to Buffalo early in the season. A veteran of two Cup-winning teams in Boston, Stanfield was a stabilizing force on a young team, plus his ability to play the point on the power play added more punch to the Sabres lineup. He shared his memories of the Finals: "I thought we had the better team as far as skills. It just happened that Bernie Parent came up large for them and we couldn't put it by him. It was an interesting series. I still feel if we go back we could have changed a few things, but I played with a fractured ankle all the way through, so I couldn't help the team as much as I would have if I hadn't had that injured ankle. I couldn't skate properly, but I did play the six games. It was unfortunate after getting there by beating Montreal; that series [versus Montreal] was just unbelievable. I thought that was as close as we could come to winning the Stanley Cup because when we landed at Niagara Falls Airport it brought back so many more memories of me playing in Boston. All the fans showed up at the airport, and that was like winning the Stanley Cup, beating Montreal. And then we had to play Philadelphia."

Jim Schoenfeld thinks Stanfield was key to pulling the team

together for the run at the Cup. "We all had a kind of higher regard for one another and what we brought to the table, and because of that I think we pulled together more as a team. Then Freddie came to the team. He was a terrific addition, not only as a player but as a friend. We used to drive to the games and practices together all the time. Lucky me, I get Horty [Tim Horton] as a mentor, then I get Freddie Stanfield. You talk about the beginning of a blessed career.

"Freddie showed me how important it was to do things away from the ice, the players and the girlfriends and the wives. He pulled us together and we had a close-knit team, so we all got along great and all liked each other, and we became close."

But Schoenfeld doesn't have fond memories of the Final against Philadelphia: "I never looked at it as a triumph or just a good thing. We beat other teams a lot that year. It feels good to get there, but you get there to win. I don't play anymore, so I can't fill that void, but that's life. The funny thing is that I was captain of the team at that time, and I thought we had such a good team; we're going to be here for the next three to four years in a row. We never did. We got to the semis in '79–'80 and that's the closest we ever got. We came up against some good teams, and the thing I remember in the '79–'80 playoff series, [is] losing to Long Island. I remember losing one in overtime and the Islanders went on to win the series, beating Philly in the Final. It was the first of four Cups [for the Islanders], and you wonder if we had somehow been able to pull that series out, and maybe gone on to beat Philly, but who knows. There are a lot of *if*s. But would that have been the first of four? You know, you get that close and it is close. There's such a fine line. I've learned that there is such a fine line between winning and losing. And sometimes it is hard to define. But there they were, the New York Islanders, and they did this and beat Philly, the first of four, a dynasty."

Jim Lorentz has yet another point of view: "It was a huge disappointment to lose to Philadelphia, especially in our own building. We had never been able to play well in Philadelphia, and that just killed us in the series. I thought there were a couple of major points. We were outcoached in that series. We made very few adjustments. I thought Philadelphia made many adjustments. They did a good job against the Perreault line. Plus goaltending was much better on Philadelphia's side. Bernie Parent was the Conn Smythe winner and rightly so. As I reflect back, I realize you seldom get opportunities to go that far. As a young player you don't realize that. As a young player in my first full year I had gone to the Finals. I thought that this may be a regular occurrence. But it doesn't happen very often. When you get there, you have to take full advantage. We just didn't do it. We fell short for many reasons."

The Olympians

The story of the 1980 U.S. Hockey Team that competed and won the Olympic gold medal has been told and retold, with two movies on the subject. Broadcaster Al Michaels has made a career based on his call of the final moments of the U.S. victory over the Soviet Union in the Olympic semifinals. There are few American hockey fans who don't get a chill when they watch one of the movies that tell the story of Coach Herb Brooks and his band of gifted college players and amateurs who brought the Soviet team to earth in that marvelous display of true grit versus professional power.

In case you forgot, or didn't know, the United States had assembled this team of college kids and a few who had graduated to face the rest of the world in the Olympic Games at Lake Placid, New York. The Yankees were a good amateur team, and the Soviets were a squad made up of the best in their hockey system, amateurs in name but professionals in game. They were paid to play and the world knew it.

Somehow, the Americans were able to cobble together a competitive team, which was more than their Canadian counterparts could do.

But they didn't compete at all with the Soviets in a game in New York a few days before the Olympic tournament began. The Americans were blown off the ice by a 10–3 score. Watching the game was painful for the crowd at Madison Square Garden. I was on hand and thought there was no way the U.S. team could beat the powerful Soviet team, anchored by Vladislav Tretiak in goal. A year earlier, I had been part of the TV production team for the Soviet-NHL Challenge Cup Series at Madison Square Garden in New York, and watched the Russians easily beat the NHL All-Star unit in a deciding, 6–0 shutout.

The boys from Minnesota with their home-grown coach had no chance. They were out of their league, we thought. (Most of the U.S. players were products of Minnesota and college hockey there. Their coach, Herb Brooks, had the same pedigree.) However, the U.S. team won in a semifinal meeting with the Soviets, 4–3. It was and still is the greatest moment in the history of American hockey and American prowess in the Olympics. The final "Do you believe in miracles?" call by ABC's Al Michaels is a part of the American lexicon. The Sabres tried to catch part of the miracle in a bottle.

The Boys from Minnesota

Mike Ramsey, a lanky defenseman from the University of Minnesota, had been the first draft choice of Buffalo's Scotty Bowman in the June 1979 amateur draft, now called the entry draft by the NHL, a league that is known for changing the names of its divisions, its conferences, and its awards at whim.

There was nothing whimsical about Ramsey. He was considered by many to be one of the best defensive prospects in the world. Bowman wanted him for the Sabres, but Ramsey chose to join the U.S. Olympic team, which was to train all fall and through winter up to the Games in Lake Placid. A year before Bowman tapped Ramsey, he had selected center Rob McClanahan, another University of Minnesota player, in the draft's third round. McClanahan also was invited to join the U.S. team, and along with he and Ramsey were Minnesota natives Eric Strobel and John Harrington.

After the United States beat Finland 4–2 to win the gold medal, Bowman swooped in on the players (and their agents) as only Scotty can swoop. The Sabres were leaving on a four-game road trip, and Bowman announced quietly that the quartet from the U.S. team would be with the Sabres on that trip. Suddenly, after a season of practicing and playing under Herb Brooks, the tension and the thrills of best in international play, and an American public in love with their hockey team more than their hockey, four tired young men found themselves in the big leagues.

So where did Scotty begin driving them as hard as Scotty always drove his players?

To poolside in a plush Newport Beach, California, resort hotel. For three and a half days, in the middle of a busy NHL season, Bowman took his team to lotus land, where they bused to practice each day and then spent the rest of the time golfing, sunning, playing tennis, and just plain loafing. McClanahan said he "couldn't believe the NHL would be this great," when he was asked his impression by a journalist along on the trip. "Don't worry," he was told, "it won't last very long."

Ramsey moved right into the Sabres defensive rotation. McClanahan also got regular duty at center on the Sabres' third or fourth line. Harrington and Strobel, meanwhile, were sent the next week to Rochester of the AHL, where they had brief careers before exiting pro hockey. They sure had the best of times for a few days when they first became pros.

Chapter 15
Drafts and Trades Change the Team

"I really grew in exhibition games a lot and was fortunate enough to be on the big club the first year...It was a growing process. There is no other place that I would have rather broken in than Buffalo."

–Phil Housley

Wowie Howie—Phil Housley—was the Sabres high-scoring defenseman in the 1980s.

Wowie Howie

Scotty Bowman wasn't used to losing at any level, what with his string of Stanley Cups in Montreal, his success as a coach of the St. Louis Blues in the league's first expansion, and his runs in the playoffs during his first seasons in Buffalo. He had come to Buffalo as both general manager and coach, but turned over the bench duties to Roger Neilson in his second season, 1980–81. Scotty assumed the coaching gig again in 1981–82 after Neilson left to coach the Vancouver Canucks. Scotty's first teams had been winners of the Adams Division during the regular season but didn't get any further than the Stanley Cup semifinals in the spring of 1980, losing to the eventual Cup champion New York Islanders in six games.

General Manager Bowman had stockpiled draft choices. When the time to pick from the best young players arrived in June of 1982, Bowman could use the first two rounds to start a rebuilding job on his aging Sabres team.

With the sixth overall pick Scotty selected a choirboy in appearance who turned out to be one of the greatest U.S.-born players in the history of the NHL. Cherub-cheeked Phil Housley was all of 18 years old on draft day and hardly appeared that old. But he was already playing like a man.

"I knew there were a lot of scouts following me in my junior year of high school in St. Paul, Minnesota," Housley recalled. "I had a taste of playing professionally at the World National Championship Games with the National Team. In 1982 I tried out and they gave me a couple of games. After an exhibition game in Germany I was told I made the team. And at that time I was playing against a lot of pros, the Red Army Team, against Wayne Gretzky and Bobby Clarke, and I thought I was pretty good.

"I didn't know where I was going to go in the draft. There was speculation I was going to go first round, ninth pick, but Scotty Bowman chose me sixth pick overall. I was excited. I think that time at the world championships sort of made my decision for me; if I was going to college or signing a letter of intent and going straight to pro. Buffalo signed me and had me come to my first camp. I made the team and it was great, and that's the history.

"My agent told me that when he talked to Scotty that I might have to spend some time in the minors, and that scared the death out of me, so I really worked hard that summer, training. I came into camp in excellent shape. I think I was one of the top two or three who were in shape, and I had a pretty good camp. The exhibition season went along and I think I was right up there with Gilbert Perreault. I really grew in exhibition games a lot and was fortunate enough to be on the big club the first year."

Housley was just out of high school and moving to another state—and another world.

"It was a growing process. There is no other place that I would have rather broken in than Buffalo. The guys were great and really made me feel comfortable, and they taught me how to be a pro. Lindy Ruff, Mike Ramsey, Larry Playfair, and Gilbert Perreault all really went out of their way to make me feel comfortable, and that made me feel part of the team. One example: in the first exhibition game, we faced Montreal. Guy Lafleur was my idol growing up and here I was, in the first exhibition game of the 1982 season, circling at center ice for warm-ups, my back was sometimes touching Lafleur's back. It's a great memory.

"I was named third star that game, so from that point I felt that I belonged to the team in a league with the best players in the world."

Hazing

Housley was a rookie when the veteran players in the NHL conducted a hazing ritual that Phil wouldn't describe. "Hazing was a tradition in Buffalo," he said. "They did something that I don't want to speak of and I want to keep that behind closed doors, but that's just part of coming together as a team. Now they do it a lot differently; the rookies take the veteran players out for dinner."

Today's NHL rosters are composed of players from more than North America, and Housley believes that's the reason the old form of hazing has disappeared.

"I can't imagine the same thing happening today. These guys wouldn't stand for it," he said.

So what was the hazing tradition that Housley didn't want to identify? Simply put, a group of teammates would wrestle a rookie onto his back on a training table, and out would come the shaving cream and a safety razor. They'd pull down the rookie's pants and shorts and lather him up in an area that usually doesn't get shaved. The more a rookie would struggle, the bigger chance that safety razor wouldn't be so safe. Once they were trapped, the rookies usually quieted down and accepted they wouldn't be hirsute there for a while.

The same tradition had been going on in Canadian junior hockey for years, and as rookies became veterans in the NHL they were expected to apply the hazing technique to the next wave of rookies coming into the club. Once you were in the NHL, even when you were traded to another team as a rookie (which seldom happened), you didn't have to go through the ritual again.

Coaches and Technique

Housley was one of the first players to make the NHL at the age of 18, and he is still one of the few. He was a work in progress as far as his knowledge of game tactics was concerned. He reflected on the coaches he had who influenced him most and why they were successful.

"I think being able to motivate and push your buttons and know all the players' personalities," he said. "In today's game, it's a different teaching process. Back then, Scotty taught me a lot about the game and how he motivated players. He kept you on edge, so you never felt comfortable, but he got the most out of you. I learned a lot about the mental part of the game as well as the tactical part of the game from Scotty.

"The game evolved when the trap came in. Everyone is playing so well positionally, so I think that's another teaching process. I think Brian Sutter was a great guy who could motivate you. He became a really great coach toward the end of my career.

I've had a lot of great coaches. You just try and take a piece from every coach and try to apply it to games. There are so many great coaches that I had. I think a couple of things Scotty Bowman and Brian Sutter did had a lot to do with my success."

Housley sometimes played forward, mostly on the power play. "I didn't have any problem adjusting to different positions. To be a really good power play specialist, you have to know all the positions on the power play," he said. "It didn't matter where you were put, you know the role of that position. And to go back to my high school coach, he taught me a lot about the power play, and I just tried to use that in my first year.

"I played a little bit as a center, too. Nowadays, and back then, you're almost that third defenseman back in the zone. So I knew how to play defense, and I knew how to support and position myself. It was just like adding another defenseman to the zone, trying to break out. You didn't need any adjustment. I just had the skills to play that position, but I thought I saw the game better when everything was right in front of me at defense."

The Foligno Leap

The biggest trade in Sabres history was triggered by Scotty Bowman on December 2, 1981. He sent Danny Gare, Derek Smith, and Jim Schoenfeld to Detroit for Dale McCourt, Brent Peterson, and Mike Foligno.

Buffalo fans were astounded at first. Schoenfeld had been a captain of the Sabres. So had Gare. They were two of the stars who had established Buffalo as a league power in the mid-1970s. Another, French Connection left winger Rick Martin, had been traded in March of the same year.

Foligno had been nearly a star in Detroit. He was runner-up in the voting for the Calder Trophy as Rookie of the Year in his first season, tallying 36 goals. In his second season he scored 28 more, and his aggressive play and quickness made him a dangerous opponent.

"It was a shocker to me when it happened," Foligno

Getty Images

Mike Foligno would leap in exultation after scoring a goal.

recalled. "I didn't realize that they were even thinking of moving me, a younger guy on the team with Detroit. I'd been part of a rebuild to go with younger players and I had just come off some pretty good years.

"I was excited when I realized it was Buffalo. It was a little closer to home [Sudbury, Ontario], and there were a couple of great people in Buffalo I had kind of grown up watching. One of them was Gilbert Perreault. I was definitely excited to have the opportunity to come into Buffalo and play with a player like Gilbert. The other one was Scotty Bowman. I felt that it was going to be a pretty good opportunity for me to learn from one of the best coaches in the game."

Foligno's style won over the hearts of Buffalo hockey fans in just a few games. He often went into the corners hell-bent-for-leather and usually came out standing. His feisty play, size, and devil-may-care attitude were attractive traits to the Aud crowd, who had lost Schoenfeld and Gare, both hard-nosed players themselves. But it was Foligno's exuberance after he scored a goal that sealed the deal. He went airborne.

"Jumping in the air after I scored was just something I did automatically," he said. "It was a celebratory dance. Whether you're a football player in the end zone or a baseball player and you hit a home run, everybody does something. That was my thing. It was automatic and it had nothing to do with rubbing it in the nose of the other team. More or less, it was just a show of my jubilation for scoring a goal."

Foligno had many chances to practice his joyous leap. He played 1,018 regular-season games in the NHL and scored 355 times, 247 of them in a Sabres uniform. There is a generation of hockey fans who grew up on the Niagara Frontier whose best memory of the Sabres was the Foligno leap when he scored.

Scotty Knew His Stuff

The numbers speak for Scotty Bowman: most wins as a coach, nine Stanley Cups, championships and All-Star Teams wherever he coached. But how does Foligno evaluate the coach/GM he played for in Buffalo?

"I think he was all about the game," Foligno said. "You can learn a lot of things from him because he's walked the walk. He's been his own guy, a player in the game, biding his time waiting for the opportunity to help out as an assistant coach and on to being the head coach, then the management field. He had opportunities to do that, as well as scouting. I'm sure a lot of teams today in all different organizations in the league have called Scotty to pick his brain.

"If there's any way to grow the game, Scotty will be there to help grow the game, and that's something he's always done. He went to St. Louis, Montreal...a place like St. Louis, a midwest state, in the first expansion. His Blues brought a higher level of play to a bigger market in the United States. You know, I think Scotty and the Blues are part of the mystique of how hockey started to grow in the United States.

"As I look back on it, I have a whole different perspective of what was going on. I have a broader picture in my mind as to what needs to be done to bring a championship to a city. I've had a whole bunch of years to look back on it, to see what actually happened behind the scenes because I'm removed from the situation.

"I know that there was a lot of pressure in Buffalo to bring a winner during Perreault's tenure there, and they wanted to see Gilbert win a Stanley Cup. The first couple of years I was there, we had some great opportunities to win. The first year against the Boston Bruins, we went to the seventh game in overtime. I think it was Brad Park who scored the goal to beat us. I actually feel had we won that overtime against Boston in that seventh game, we would have won the Stanley Cup. We definitely had the team that could do it. We had the goaltending. We had the fans. We had everything in our favor. I remember like it was yesterday. Unfortunately, a bounced shot went the other way. If you get through the first couple of rounds, there are tough spells, and then all of a sudden the team gains confidence and momentum and you're sailing. What Scotty had built was coming together, and a bad bounce in that overtime forced the tide to turn the other way."

Foligno has worked his way through various professional coaching jobs since his playing days ended, and he is currently GM and coach of the Ontario Hockey League Sudbury Wolves, a junior club. He has one son in his first year on the junior Wolves roster, and another son, Nick, who was a first-round pick in the 2006 entry draft. Nick made the lineup of the Ottawa Senators in his first pro season. Born in Buffalo, Nick made a Foligno goal celebration jump when he notched his first in the NHL in the fall of 2007.

"Obviously it was something he wanted to do, and I'm very proud of him for thinking about me. It wasn't something he had to do. It was a pretty nice thing, and I'll never forget it."

Bert Revisited

The first 17 years of the Buffalo Sabres encompassed the career of the franchise's greatest player—Perreault—and its two greatest hockey executives, Scotty Bowman and the late Punch Imlach. Each of them is a member of the Hall of Fame, and each made a unique contribution to the history of the league.

As a player, Gilbert Perreault may have been the most exciting player end-to-end of all time. He could pick up the puck behind his net and go the distance with almost mesmerizing speed and moves. In the end he was more liable to pass off to a French Connection winger for the goal than to score it himself.

His native tongue is French and to this day he resides in his hometown of Victoriaville, Quebec. Bert's English is fine, but spoken with a heavy French accent. He's proud of his French heritage and lives in a French-speaking world.

One night, early in his career, Perreault's intense drive to win was revealed to his teammates in a way that they found both humorous and noteworthy. In the Buffalo dressing room before a playoff game against Montreal, Bert and his mates sat waiting for the final buzzer that would summon them onto the ice to play the "Flying Frenchmen," the most fabled franchise in hockey.

Tension hung in the air, as the Sabres sat on the edges of their locker seats, hunched over in nervous anticipation. No one spoke. Then Perreault rose to his feet and said, "Let's go beat those [bleeping] frogs," and he headed for the exit mat leading to Memorial Auditorium ice. As he often did, Perreault let his play do the rest of the talking. The Sabres beat the Canadiens to wrap up a Stanley Cup series, and Bert was the first star.

Bert has only fond memories of his career in Buffalo and counts 1975 as the top memory of them all. "Punch did an excellent job. In five years we were in the Finals," he said. "We had some great draft picks with him in charge. He also made some

Gilbert Perrault, mixing it up with Bobby Clarke of the Flyers, in 1975.

great trades. We got Don Luce in a trade. He meant so much to the team. We got Rene Robert in a trade, too."

Perreault never felt he had to be the superstar if the new Sabres franchise was to be a success, despite his selection first overall in the draft. "I had to prove to them that it was not a mistake," he said. "But the pressure was not all on me. It was on all of us that were picked in those first few drafts. That's how you build a team. The pressure was on all of us for the first five years, not just on me."

In his 17-year stint in Buffalo, Bert had only two hockey bosses, Imlach and Bowman. "They were top men to have in the job—tough—but top men," he said.

Today Perreault counts himself as "retired" but still works for the Sabres in a public relations capacity and spends several weeks a year on the job in Buffalo.

No one who ever saw him play can forget the increasing crowd noise—from a buzz to a roar—as Perreault streaked up the ice with the puck. For 17 seasons, he was worth the price of admission.

Imlach Redux

George Imlach was the old NHL. He didn't believe in player agents and only grudgingly accepted them. He had never gotten beyond senior hockey as a player, but that was a time when senior hockey in Canada was darn good, as there were only six teams in the NHL, with 16 players each. Imlach got his nickname in hockey because someone said he skated like an NHL player of an even earlier era, Punch Broadbent.

That was the way it was in the old NHL. Tradition was the most important element of the game. There were no high-priced marketing departments, no "sales consultants" pumping season tickets with incessant phone calls, no advertising pasted on every available surface, and no corporate boxes with wine and cheese.

Imlach grew up in a hockey world that was rigid in its protocols, unfair to its players who were treated much like serfs, and a closed loop confined to Canada and four U.S. cities. There were no Russians, Czechs, or Swedes on any hockey horizon. Canadian boys wanted to become Canadian men good enough to play in the NHL, and they became a community hero—an icon—if they succeeded. Even getting a chance to play pro hockey was an honor bestowed on very few. There just weren't that many jobs.

Punch combined a fierce competitive fire with a canny businessman's acuity. He not only played senior hockey but he also invested in it and soon ended up owning part of the senior team in Quebec City. In the next few years he upped the ante, buying into Vancouver in the old Western Hockey League (pro) with his close friend Joe Crozier and the legendary hockey broadcaster, Foster Hewitt.

During his years in Quebec, Imlach had the services of Jean Beliveau, who was paid a king's ransom at the time to stay in senior hockey, rather than turn pro with the Canadiens. Beliveau was the best player in the world who wasn't in the NHL, and Imlach learned that a franchise could be built around the special skills of a superstar. Later, he believed Perreault could do the same thing for Buffalo as Beliveau did for Quebec and then Montreal. He was correct. Perreault would energize the fans in Buffalo from the beginning. The city had been a very successful franchise in the American Hockey League, even winning the AHL playoff championship the season before the Sabres entered the picture. Many fans were skeptical about an NHL expansion franchise versus a top-level AHL club, and they showed it at the box office the first quarter of Buffalo's initial big-league season. There were hardly any sellouts even though Memorial Auditorium held only 10,400 before its roof was raised.

Imlach's good fortune in the spin of a carnival wheel had brought Perreault to Buffalo. As his coach, Punch gave Perreault all the freedom to roam and play offensively that Gilbert wanted. Straight out of junior, Perreault was spectacular. He could bring fans out of their seats with his end-to-end rushes. His talents brought fans into those seats as the season progressed, with sellouts the rule rather than the exception by the season's midpoint. Perreault was a big minus player as a rookie, but he became a solid plus player for the rest of his career.

Punch had worked in the American League before getting a shot as an assistant GM in Toronto in 1958. The Leafs had an arcane management structure—a committee called the Silver Seven—that ran the franchise, and Imlach learned that political skills as well as hockey knowledge were needed to succeed in his new job. In his nine-year stay with Toronto, he took the Leafs to something that hasn't happened since, a Stanley Cup in 1967.

Imlach was stubborn, demanding, and cocky. He was also shrewd and canny and had a wild sense of humor that few knew about. In his first year with Buffalo, Punch was writing a weekly column on hockey for the *Toronto Star*. The column was ghostwritten and edited by his close friend, the late *Star* sports editor, Scott Young (father of singer Neil Young). Phil Esposito was at the zenith of his NHL career in Boston that season, converting goals on the vaunted Bruins offense like no power play specialist ever had done before.

One week Punch devoted his column to Esposito, writing that he "certainly would like to have" Espo in Buffalo. After reading the article I decided to have a little fun with Punch with some help from his secretary. In those days all official NHL business was conducted using a teletype machine, an ancient sort of typewriter that could be used to send and receive printed messages by telephone wire connection. It was easy to write something on the machine but not send it; just print it. I arranged for a printed message addressed to Punch from the president of the NHL, Clarence Campbell. The alleged message from the top told Imlach he was being fined $5,000 for tampering. The "tampering" alleged in the fake message was because Imlach had written that he wanted to have Esposito in Buffalo. This, the message said, was in direct contravention of the league's rules.

Signed: Clarence Campbell, President.

When Punch read the message placed on his desk with some other paperwork, he exploded, yelling to his secretary, a now-very-nervous Dory Urbanick, to "get that SOB Campbell on the phone."

At that point I figured the joke had gone on long enough and rushed in to tell Punch it was only a gag. Imlach stared at me for a long time, tipped his beaver fedora back on his bald head, and said: "Get him anyway, Dory. I've got a free pass to tell that SOB what I think of him, and when it's all over I can blame it on Wieland." Fortunately, Dory reported that Campbell wasn't in his office that day. She really saved her boss and the PR man by faking the call.

Scotty

It's remarkable that two of the seminal figures in the history of the NHL never played in the league. Imlach capped out by attending a Detroit Red Wings training camp after serving in the

Canadian forces during World War II, then moving on to senior hockey in Quebec.

Scotty Bowman's promising hockey career as a player ended when he was struck in the head in a junior game. The injury was severe and the young Montreal native turned to coaching to stay in the game he loved. By the age of 22, he was the coach in Ottawa of the Junior Canadiens in the Quebec league, tasting his first big championship there. He moved to Peterborough in the OHA and jumped into the NHL in first expansion in 1967 as an assistant to Lynn Patrick with St. Louis. Patrick decided to quit coaching shortly after and at age 34, Scotty was head coach of the Blues.

His record is astonishing in these days of short coaching careers and burnout. He won five Stanley Cups with the Montreal Canadiens, three with Detroit, and another with Pittsburgh. In St. Louis, his Blues reached the Stanley Cup Finals three times. Scotty has won more games as a coach—1,467 including play-offs—than anyone in hockey history. Only during his time in Buffalo was there no Stanley Cup parade at least one spring day.

Some observers of the Buffalo years say that Scotty was plagued by a combination of bad luck and bad fortune, the latter referring to the declining dollars available from the Knox brothers and other team investors. This meant Bowman was unable to spend for player help when he needed it to turn the Sabres from a good team into a Cup-winning team. Others have said Scotty was so used to being a coach that he was pulled between his success at that job and the requirements of being a general manager. Witness the fact that he hired and fired coaches regularly in Buffalo, and usually replaced an old coach with a new but familiar one—himself.

Hanging out with Scotty to this day is like being in the middle of an encyclopedia. Not just a hockey encyclopedia, but a general knowledge tome. His mind seems to always operate in high gear. Plus he has an ironic sense of humor that confounds listeners. An example: When he was with Buffalo the Sabres supplied the roster of an AHL farm club 60 miles down the road in Rochester.

The Americans were in desperate straits late one season, with nearly every defenseman out injured. Buffalo had no players it could assign from the NHL, and there was nobody available from the lower minors. Bowman knew of one guy, who shall remain nameless. A big, raw, and aggressive player, this defenseman had played in the AHL before and had become the Amerks' all-time single-season penalty leader.

He was not as good a player as a fighter, so his pro career had seemingly ended with an outright release.

Bowman called him on the phone: "So, what are you doing with yourself these days," he asked the player. The reply indicated the player was working regularly for a Buffalo company.

"How would you like to play hockey again?" asked Bowman. "Do you still have your skates?" he asked, turning to those in his office with a real twinkle in his eye. The conversation continued and Scotty made a pay deal, told the player to pack up and head off to Rochester. "One thing," Bowman said. "Don't quit your day job."

Paul Wieland (left) and Rick Jeanneret call the action on cable television in 1972.

About the Author

Paul Wieland joined the Buffalo Sabres in the first few months of the new franchise in 1970 and spent more than 25 years there as public relations director, communications director, and executive producer of television sports for the Sabres cable network and for a TV station owned by the hockey team. He also served as a practice goalie for many years.

Wieland has worked as a producer or director for Sportschannel America, a producer for coverage of Russian/NHL summit series, and for regional networks including Empire and The NHL TV Network. He most recently worked as a television producer and director of college basketball for ESPN and other regional sports networks.

He was a reporter for two Buffalo dailies, the *Buffalo Evening News* and the *Buffalo Courier-Express*. He won a combined 31 national and regional awards for news, features, and science reporting.

He is a professor in the Jandoli School of Journalism at St. Bonaventure University in upstate New York and is at work on a satirical novel about the pro sports business.